What Teachers
REALLY
need to know about
Formative
Assessment

WhatTeachers
REALLY
need to know about
Formative
Assessment

Laura Greenstein

Alexandria, Virginia USA

ASCD®

1703 N. Beauregard St. • Alexandria, VA 22311-1714 USA
Phone: 800-933-2723 or 703-578-9600 • Fax: 703-575-5400
Web site: www.ascd.org • E-mail: member@ascd.org
Author guidelines: www.ascd.org/write

Gene R. Carter, *Executive Director;* Judy Zimny, *Chief Program Development Officer;* Nancy Modrak, *Publisher;* Scott Willis, *Director, Book Acquisitions & Development;* Genny Ostertag, *Acquisitions Editor;* Julie Houtz, *Director, Book Editing & Production;* Katie Martin, *Editor;* Catherine Guyer, *Senior Graphic Designer;* Mike Kalyan, *Production Manager;* Barton Matheson Willse & Worthington, *Typesetter;* Sarah Plumb, *Production Specialist*

Printed in the United States of America. Cover art © 2010 by ASCD. ASCD publications present a variety of viewpoints. The views expressed or implied in this book should not be interpreted as official positions of the Association.

All Web links in this book are correct as of the publication date below but may have become inactive or otherwise modified since that time. If you notice a deactivated or changed link, please e-mail books@ascd.org with the words "Link Update" in the subject line. In your message, please specify the Web link, the book title, and the page number on which the link appears.

PAPERBACK ISBN: 978-1-4166-0996-4   ASCD product #110017   n6/10

Also available as an e-book (see Books in Print for the ISBNs).

Quantity discounts for the paperback edition only: 10–49 copies, 10%; 50+ copies, 15%; for 1,000 or more copies, call 800-933-2723, ext. 5634, or 703-575-5634. For desk copies: member@ascd.org.

Library of Congress Cataloging-in-Publication Data

Greenstein, Laura.
    What teachers really need to know about formative assessment / Laura Greenstein.
        p. cm.
    Includes bibliographical references and index.
    ISBN 978-1-4166-0996-4 (pbk. : alk. paper)   1. Educational tests and measurements.   I. Title.
    LB3051.G72 2010
    371.26'4—dc22
                                                                                    2010008217

20 19 18 17 16 15 14 13 12   2 3 4 5 6 7 8 9 10 11 12

What Teachers REALLY need to know about Formative Assessment

Preface

The educational process is one of continual reorganization, reconstruction, transforming . . . since in reality there is nothing to which growth is relative save more growth, there is nothing to which education is subordinate, save more education.

—John Dewey

When asked, "What do you want to be when you grow up?" young children don't typically say they want to become a psychometrician or school administrator. Yet people who have made assessment their career have had their inspirations and can point to the eye-opening experiences, wondrous events, or extraordinary individuals that have influenced them along the way.

My father started me on my path. He dropped out of school at age 12, when his mother died, and went to work to support his family. As an adult, he finished his high school education at night school and always extolled the value of a good education. His influence helped me to become a lifelong learner, and I routinely and robustly impart that message to my children.

From my extended family, I have learned the value of *sisu*, a Finnish word meaning "perseverance," and I have also learned to embrace a family tradition of questioning and testing hypotheses. These two values have stood me in good stead throughout my career. I like to question and entertain different viewpoints and persevere in doing so until I reach a balanced conclusion. You will see I have kept to this in the book by including other researchers' opinions on issues, which are at times divergent.

When I started working in education in the 1970s, I brought my bent for questioning to the era's largely homogeneous classrooms, with their straight rows of student desks and teachers standing in front of the room talking at students. During that time, I proposed a master's thesis on the relationship between classroom seating arrangements, instructional methods, and learning outcomes. My hypothesis was that flexible seating arrangements would be more conducive to discussion and collaboration. My academic advisors discouraged me from this focus, opining that it was not important enough to warrant research, but my interest in the relationship between teaching practice and learning outcomes persisted.

At the ripe age of 50, I became passionate about assessment. In my avid reading of educational journals and research (my father's influence, I'm sure), I began to see a clear connection between what we know about *how* students learn (based on a large body of research on cognition) and the development of strategies that can be used to accurately determine *what* students know. I also became aware of a significant gap between data unearthed by research and the reality of classroom practice. For example, the National Research Council's *Knowing What Students Know* (Pellegrino, Chudowsky, & Glaser, 2001), a fundamental volume on contemporary assessment issues, is one of this topic area's best-kept secrets. It shows a clear discrepancy between how students learn and how teachers measure learning outcomes. Understanding by Design, an instructional design system presented by Grant Wiggins and Jay McTighe in a 1998 book of the same name, has been promoted for over a decade, yet many teachers have still not heard of it. D. Royce Sadler's (1989) work on formative assessment provided a foundation for the Black and Wiliam (1998) landmark study that led to further research on the value of formative assessment. But as Rick Stiggins (2002) has noted, the follow-up and application of this knowledge is sorely lacking. These ideas developed into a dissertation topic and a new twist in my career. A passion found at any age is a gift. As the famous philosopher Georg Wilhelm Friedrich Hegel said, "We may affirm absolutely that nothing great in the world has been accomplished without passion."

During the course of my dissertation, members of my graduate cohort were a valuable support and source of inspiration. Many of them were also formalizing their areas of interest, developing hypotheses, and designing research studies, and much of their work related to assessment. For example, Marguerite was examining how schools select reading programs to meet the needs of their early learners. Bernie was looking at the criteria that districts used in the principal selection process. Kathy was studying programs for at-risk students and investigating the success rates of a variety of programs.

Most recently, my inspiration has come from teachers. I meet many in my workshops on formative assessment who are dedicated and motivated to help their students. They have steered me in new directions with their informative, illuminating, and thoughtful questions and responses. They have led me to write this book and begin to share with a broader audience the strategies I have used in my own classroom as well as ideas and inspiration from other teachers.

Maya Angelou wrote that "a bird doesn't sing because it has an answer, it sings because it has a song." In my workshops, I explain that I am not an expert with *the* answer but, rather, a maven. The word *maven* comes from a Yiddish word meaning "to understand." Malcolm Gladwell (2002) uses it in his book *The Tipping Point* to describe someone who accumulates knowledge and uses that knowledge to start a trend. Formative assessment is not a new trend, but it is gaining momentum due to the work of many mavens, many singers.

This book about assessment may more closely resemble a quilt than a song, seeing as it is stitched together from many pieces. My sister is an accomplished quilter of cloth, and although my clumsy fingers have never been up to the challenge of the fine intricacies of cutting and stitching fabric, I hope that in this book I have been a successful quilter and that a clear pattern of how to use formative assessment emerges from the pieces.

Introduction

I sometimes start a workshop by asking teachers to think back to their own student days and their *worst* assessment experience. Everyone has a story.

I've heard about tests that had nothing to do with the assigned text or the instruction. I've also heard of teachers telling students about to begin a test that they were expected to fail it. The story I often share is about my first economics class at the University of Connecticut. Having no experience with the subject and finding that the classroom lectures didn't provide much illumination, I decided my best chance to pass the test was simply to memorize portions of the text and repeat them verbatim as my answers. When the professor called me into his office to accuse me of plagiarism, I explained my predicament and, fortunately, we were both able to laugh about it. I then received some extra help in understanding economic theories and statistics. So while this was my worst test experience, it was also my first taste of the effectiveness of formative assessment, although it would be many years before I came to understand it as such.

The word *assessment* comes from the Latin root *assidere,* which means "to sit beside another." Our best assessment experiences are usually the ones that reflect the word's roots most closely; they are the times a teacher sits beside us to gather information about our progress and support our learning. The best assessments help us move forward. When my college economics professor and I finally sat side by side, he was able to understand what I did and did not know, and we were able to plan the next step together. That is formative assessment: the process of uncovering and understanding what students know in order to determine the best path to learning.

Traditional Versus Formative Assessment

The traditional way to gather information about student learning is through summative assessment—a test, sometimes teacher-generated, sometimes common across classrooms and content areas, and sometimes standardized, given at the end of instruction for the purpose of measuring achievement. As teachers, we typically use the information from our tests to assign a grade and then move on to the next unit of instruction. As administrators and policymakers, we often use scores from standardized assessments to rank our school's or district's or state's achievement. These measures are valuable. They tell us where students have placed in the race, giving us a snapshot for comparative purposes. At this point, however, the race is over. In contrast, formative assessment gives teachers information that they can use to inform their teaching and improve learning while it is in progress and while the outcome of the race can still be influenced.

Formative assessment encompasses a variety of strategies for revealing students' understanding, allowing teachers to pinpoint and address any impediments to a student's progress. The process is much like a coach setting short exercises to assess a runner's stride, speed, and equipment and then making appropriate adjustments so that the runner can improve. Teachers use formative data to decide how much and what kind of learning, support, and practice a student needs to reach the goal. When formative assessment is employed before, during, and after instruction, both teachers and students have a measure of progress.

Achievement needs to be viewed not as a test-based number but as measurable growth over time. In this context, achievement means that students are working to improve their knowledge and skills. Different students will undertake this in different ways—perhaps some taking smaller steps than others—but progress is being made nonetheless. To go back to our race analogy, runners evaluate their achievement not only by where they place in the final standings but also by how much their individual performance has improved. Formative assessment allows both teachers and students to measure learning by inches, ounces, and degrees. The results can inform teacher and student decisions about what to do next on an hour-to-hour, day-to-day, or month-to-month basis.

A Classroom View

Meet Ernesto and Mei, students in the same 9th grade pre-algebra class. Ernesto failed math in 8th grade but was promoted due to the district's policy of not retaining students. Because of budget cuts, summer school classes were not funded at his school, and his parents didn't have the resources to pay for him to be tutored elsewhere. So Ernesto is entering grade 9 as the same genial but disengaged student he has become over many years. He has found that being the class clown is an effective way to distract teachers from their work and from truly knowing his abilities.

Mei's family immigrated to this country a few years ago. She has been a reluctant learner of English, and her family and neighbors mostly speak her native language. As a student, she is well behaved, respectful, and cooperative. Her comprehension is sufficient for her to get by, but she is constrained in speaking because her verbal fluency and clarity are still limited. Intellectually, Mei is ready to study algebra, but the 8th grade teachers decided that she needed to work on her language skills in order to be successful with word problems and applying mathematical concepts.

A traditional classroom experience. Let's begin this case study comparison by imagining Ernesto and Mei in a traditional classroom. On the first day of school, their teacher, Ms. Blankenship, assigns them seats in alphabetical order and hands out a syllabus that includes topics and assignments related to the course goal: *Students will demonstrate understanding of algebra by using algebraic symbols and variables; by simplifying algebraic expressions; by solving and graphing inequalities; and by evaluating, solving, and graphing linear and quadratic equations.* As the weeks pass, Ernesto,

Mei, and their classmates all listen to the same daily lectures and receive the same homework assignments. They are all tested at the same time with the same assessments. Grades are based on an average of all summative test scores.

Mei does well with the numerical problems but has trouble with the word problems; her grades are average, and she is quiet and fairly disengaged in class. Ernesto has difficulty understanding many of the ideas in the textbook and is often baffled by the homework assignments, which he rarely completes or turns in. He begins bringing in chewed-up pieces of paper into class, joking that his hamster ate his homework. By midyear, Ms. Blankenship has a sense that Mei will be passing the class but Ernesto will not.

A formative classroom experience. In a classroom that incorporates formative assessment, Mei and Ernesto have a very different experience. On the first day of class, they take their seats at trapezoid-shaped tables that are arranged in rows. Their teacher, Mr. Major, comments that they shouldn't get too used to the seating arrangement because they'll be moving the tables around to sit in different places and with different groups and partners, depending on class activities. The students will eventually come to understand the varied groupings as their teacher's response to ongoing formative assessment data.

Mr. Major also distributes a syllabus on the first day of class that clearly states the pre-algebra course objective: *Students will demonstrate understanding of algebra by using algebraic symbols and variables; by simplifying algebraic expressions; by solving and graphing inequalities; and by evaluating, solving, and graphing linear and quadratic equations.* Because Mr. Major wants to be sure his students can relate to the lofty goal articulated in the syllabus, he attaches a handout with additional big ideas about math, such as how it is used in school, in the workplace, and in life.

Numbers can show relationships between things, Mr. Major explains. We can analyze numerical data to guide decisions, and we perform operations on numbers every day in the form of measurement, shapes, and graphs. He posts each of these purposes on large sheets of paper, distributes stacks of sticky notes, and asks the students to record some of the ways in which they use math in their daily life and attach these notes to an applicable purpose. Mei thinks of how her family struggles to make ends meet and their current calculations to figure out if they can afford to buy a car to improve their employment opportunities. On sticky notes, she writes "make a budget" and "save for a car." Ernesto tries to think of careers that don't require math but quickly realizes that the sales and service professions he was thinking of use math skills.

As the weeks pass, Mr. Major varies his instructional practices and uses pre-assessments and exercises like the sticky-notes activity and Quick-writes to get a sense of what approaches will work best for various students. For example, Mei often finds herself working in small groups where it's necessary for her to find the words to explain her mathematical reasoning. Mei realizes that when she has classmates who can clarify what the word problems mean, she is able to identify the mathematical operations necessary to come up with a solution. Initially, the idea of working with others was intimidating, but over time, Mei overcomes her shyness; working with and talking with others gets less and less intimidating.

Outgoing Ernesto relishes the opportunity to work with others. Sometimes he's grouped with other students who are struggling with the same concept that he is, and they all get directed instruction from Mr. Major; other times, the members of his group have a varied range of understanding, and they help one another learn. In this environment, Ernesto finds he doesn't feel as exposed or threatened; it's OK to admit he doesn't understand something when it's clear that others don't understand either. He also likes how the various activities in class keep things from being boring. Mr. Major doesn't just talk and assign problems; he gets everybody involved. For example, one day they all left the classroom and labeled things around the school that displayed a mathematical construct. They returned to compare and contrast the various findings, which they captured in a Venn diagram.

Mr. Major's approach also makes it easier for Ernesto, Mei, and their classmates to stay on top of the assignments. They each keep a notebook of concepts, assignments, reflections, and homework, which Mr. Major collects and reviews every three weeks and then returns with personal comments. Ernesto is especially pleased when his teacher notes his improvement in representations of algebraic expressions. He also finds suggestions and practice problems for building his capacity for evaluating algebraic expressions. Mr. Major's comments to Mei help her realize that she is very good at solving algebraic equations for the variable, and this makes her feel more confident about her abilities to tackle the new challenges when Mr. Major presents her with word problems in her folder that require her to use her English to solve them.

Even test time is different in this classroom. The reviews are student focused and include a variety of questions and summarizing strategies. Mei is very relieved when Mr. Major explains to her that she'll be able to use a translator when tackling the test's word problems. Mr. Major tells Ernesto that he'll have the opportunity to complete only as much of the test as time allows; there will be no penalty for not completing every item. Because the test is sequenced by difficulty, Ernesto feels competent until the last few questions and doesn't get discouraged or feel tempted to give up. After the test, he receives additional practice materials related to the questions he found most difficult or didn't get to. Mei receives her own customized set of follow-up materials, complete with some learning extensions and exercises that ask her to apply concepts that she understands well.

The Advantage of Formative Assessment

Research supports what we all know about teacher practice and student success: student success is largely dependent on teacher practice. Jennifer King Rice (2003) asserts, "Teacher quality matters: It is the most important school-related factor influencing student achievement" (p. 1). Marzano (2003) states that "the impact of decisions made by individual teachers is far greater than the impact of decisions made at the school and district level" (p. 71).

One of the primary functions of formative assessment is to inform instruction. By providing information about student understanding relative to goals, objectives, and standards, formative assessment helps teachers to target their instructions for greater effectiveness and make responsive instructional adjustments. In this respect, teaching and assessing are intertwined. The overlap is beneficial to students in that they regularly receive feedback in the course of learning, and it's beneficial to teachers because they regularly receive information about their teaching. With formative assessment, teaching and assessing become a cyclical process for continuous improvement, with each process informing the other (see Figure A).

When asked to describe how routine use of formative assessment affects their classroom, teachers typically observe that it

- Helps focus instruction on informed priorities
- Allows for customized learning, helping to build both basic skills and high-level learning in a way that is relevant and responsive to all learners
- Encourages teachers and students to work together toward achievement
- Increases student engagement and motivation
- Ensures grades accurately reflect students' progress toward standards
- Increases coherence between curriculum, instruction, and assessment

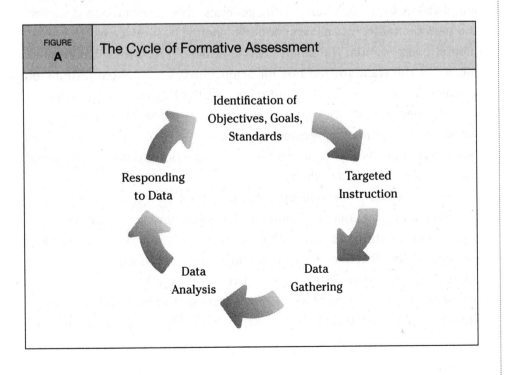

| FIGURE A | The Cycle of Formative Assessment |

The Secondary-Level Imperative

Teachers and students at both the primary and secondary levels benefit from formative assessment. Although the material in this book will be relevant to you and your students regardless of the grade you teach, I have chosen examples that emphasize formative assessment's use at the secondary level.

In elementary schools, where the instructional emphasis is on basic literacy and numeracy, teaching and tests typically align with clear curriculum standards. For example, early readers are measured on phonemic awareness, reading comprehension, and fluency. Teaching is specific to these skills, and achievement is measured through readily available measures such as DIBELS (Dynamic Indicators of Basic Early Literacy Skills). Contrast this with secondary school, where content knowledge is less explicit, and the measures are less consistent. Consider, for example, this 9th grade science benchmark in the state of Connecticut: *Understand how science and technology affect the quality of our lives.* A high school's science curriculum includes a very wide array of content, including cell structure and division, bacteria, viruses, DNA, genetics, chemistry, atomic structure, the periodic table, organic compounds, energy, heat, electricity, environmental conservation, the solar system, atmosphere, geology, and much more. Yet the standardized test for science may only have questions on sedimentary rocks, eye color, and recycling. For this reason, teachers frequently need to write their own classroom tests (Greenstein, 2005). Using formative assessment strategies can enable a school science teacher to tailor classroom assessments and teaching practices to gaps in students' mastery of the curricular goals.

But the needs of secondary schools extend far beyond curriculum, teaching, and assessment alignment. A contemporary secondary classroom includes students with widely diverse backgrounds, readiness levels, and skills. Teachers frequently must meet the needs of a class of students with a span in abilities of five or six grade levels. Formative assessment—with its emphases on pre-assessing to identify background knowledge and beliefs and on tracking individual learning—is an effective way for teachers to customize, or differentiate, content and processes to the individual student (Heritage, 2007).

Formative assessment can also help boost student engagement and potentially reduce dropout rates. The *High School Survey of Student Engagement* by the Center for Evaluation and Education Policy (2005) at Indiana University, using data from over 80,000 students in 19 states, found that less than half of students surveyed frequently discussed grades or assignments with a teacher. Almost half did not receive prompt feedback from teachers. Only 57 percent said they frequently contributed to class discussions. Half said they agree that they devote a great deal of effort to school. And only half said they get to make choices about what they study at school. Providing frequent feedback and choices to students is an essential element of formative assessment, and research shows that as students see progress in their learning and feel supported by their teacher, they often experience a positive change in motivation (Heritage, 2007).

Recommendations of studies at the middle school level center on lack of rigor and accountability in the curriculum. *Making Middle Grades Work,* from the Southern Regional Education Board (Cooney & Bottoms, 2005), concludes that middle schools need to adhere to rigorous content that is aligned with standards and develop supportive relationships that include academic support between teachers and students. Formative assessment has been shown to contribute to both achievement of standards and supportive curriculum interventions (Black, Harrison, Lee, Marshall, & Wiliam, 2003).

Preparing students for postsecondary education and for success in our swiftly changing global economy depends on fostering higher-level and critical thinking skills. The New Commission on the Skills of the American Workforce (2008) asserts that public schools are graduating students with minimal workplace competencies. The report encourages development of analytical and creative thinking skills along with the ability to interpret information and manage people. There is emerging evidence that using formative assessment in secondary classrooms can help to bridge the gap between core knowledge and the higher-level skills of analysis and application (Partnership for 21st Century Skills, 2009).

Certainly, adopting formative assessment is not a guarantee for solving every problem facing secondary schools, but it has shown strong potential for ameliorating many of them.

What Do You Know? What Do You Want to Know?

This book is a guide for incorporating formative assessment in your instructional practices. Although there is a wealth of information available about formative assessment, there is a dearth of replicable practice, particularly at the secondary level. Workshops that I have attended implore the participants to use formative assessment. Web sites cite success stories and rationales. Books provide proclamations of the importance of formative assessment. And emerging research shows that formative assessment can be an effective strategy. Less clear, however, is how to do it.

Throughout this book, I will offer practical formative assessment strategies with specific examples of their use in secondary classrooms from grades 6 to 12 in a variety of content areas. These strategies and examples are meant to help teachers navigate through formative assessment in ways that make it useful, meaningful, and relevant in helping students make measured progress toward objectives. At regular intervals throughout the text, I will also prompt readers to self-assess, reflect on practices, and apply learning.

What do you know? is the quintessential starting question of formative assessment and a good start for any type of instruction. For our purposes, the beginning question is *What do you know about formative assessment?* In answering this question, you call up your previous learning and prepare yourself to link new learning to it in pursuit of a knowledge goal. The next questions to answer are *What do you want to know that you don't know now?* and *How will go you about learning this?* Many readers will recognize this sequence of self-assessment questions as the classic K-W-L strategy, short for Know, Want to Know, Learn.

Depending on your answers to these questions, you may wish to spend more time with some parts of the book than others. If you are seeking information to help build your foundational knowledge of formative assessment, begin with Part 1. If you are looking for specific strategies to use in the classroom, you will find them in Part 2. And if your learning goal is school reform and policy issues, you will find this information in Part 3.

Please note that this book uses a language of assessment and a set of core concepts that practitioners must be familiar with in order to succeed in using formative assessment. These include definitions of core terms, such as *assessment, evaluation,* and *measurement,* as well as an understanding of the terms that are routinely used in articles and professional development resources, including *common formative assessment, validity, reliability, authentic, alternative,* and *differentiation.* Appendix A offers a set of definitions derived from my own work and the synthesis of conventional wisdom. Depending on your degree of familiarity with assessment, you may decide to review this glossary before reading further. Appendix B provides a quick reference to a number of formative assessment strategies, including those I discuss in the text.

I hope that this book provides some of what you're looking for in terms of learning, but I also encourage you to explore other resources given in the text and listed in the References section if a topic strikes you as one you wish to explore in more depth.

PART 1

Building
Foundations

- How does formative assessment differ from summative assessment?
- What makes assessment formative? Is it the strategies used, when the strategies are used, or how the teacher applies assessment data?
- Is formative assessment appropriate in some subject areas but not others?
- What can we learn from foundational studies and reports on formative assessment, especially those published by Rick Stiggins and Paul Black and Dylan Wiliam?

Your turn: Take a quick glance at the material in this part of the book and write two other questions that immediately come to mind.

This section of the book focuses on the base knowledge that will support a conceptual shift from traditional assessment to formative assessment and its various strategies. Understanding the theory behind formative assessment practice will help you make sound decisions about using it.

Chapter 1 presents formative assessment's key principles, illustrated with some samples from classroom practice, and provides a brief history of formative assessment's development. Chapter 2 focuses on the answers to the most commonly asked questions about formative assessment.

CHAPTER 1

The Fundamentals of Formative Assessment

This chapter looks at the essential principles of formative assessment and provides a preview of best practice. Our focus here is both the content and context of formative assessment: its basic elements and some of the reasons it has risen to prominence and gained support as an effective means of improving student learning.

Essential Principles

The information in this section has been gathered from numerous sources and aligned around three significant concepts: (1) formative assessment is student focused, (2) formative assessment is instructionally informative, and (3) formative assessment is outcomes based.

In an effort not to duplicate information available in other resources, I have condensed the elements and their definitions quite a bit. If you would like to read more about the fundamentals of formative assessment, I recommend "Working Inside the Black Box" (Black, Harrison, Lee, Marshall, &

Wiliam, 2004); *Classroom Assessment for Student Learning: Doing It Right— Using It Well* (Stiggins, Arter, Chappuis, & Chappuis, 2004); and *Classroom Assessment and Grading That Work* (Marzano, 2006).

Formative Assessment Is Student Focused

Formative assessment is purposefully directed toward the student. It does not emphasize how teachers deliver information but, rather, how students receive that information, how well they understand it, and how they can apply it. With formative assessment, teachers gather information about their students' progress and learning needs and use this information to make instructional adjustments. They also show students how to accurately and honestly use self-assessments to improve their own learning. Instructional flexibility and student-focused feedback work together to build confident and motivated learners.

In brief: Formative assessment helps teachers

• Consider each student's learning needs and styles and adapt instruction accordingly

• Track individual student achievement

• Provide appropriately challenging and motivational instructional activities

• Design intentional and objective student self-assessments

• Offer all students opportunities for improvement

In practice: Students in Mrs. Chavez's English class are studying character development. They have read about Scout in *To Kill a Mockingbird* and Holden Caulfield in *The Catcher in the Rye*.

Early in the unit, Mrs. Chavez asks her students to define a character trait and give an example of someone in literature or in real life who demonstrates that trait. She gathers their examples in a list, which she posts in the classroom. This is valuable information about the starting point for the unit: in this case, it helps the teacher determine whether she needs to clarify the concept of character traits or can move on with the application of character traits to literature.

Based on the data her students provide, Mrs. Chavez decides to move forward. She arranges the class into random groups and asks each group to write all the character traits of Scout that they can think of on individual yellow sticky notes—one trait per note—and then do the same for Holden Caulfield, this time using blue sticky notes. Then each group posts their responses on the original list of traits, alongside each character trait. Areas of agreement and disagreement are discussed. Mrs. Chavez uses a questioning strategy to elicit information and to clarify any lingering gaps in understanding or accuracy. Following this, students work on their own to create a T chart for each character, using the left side of the T to list life experiences and challenges and the right side to list how these factors have influenced traits and behaviors. Note that Mrs. Chavez has done very little lecturing or whole-class teaching to this point, making for a very student-focused lesson.

Formative Assessment Is Instructionally Informative

During instruction, teachers assess student understanding and progress toward standards mastery in order to evaluate the effectiveness of their instructional design. Both teachers and students, individually and together, review and reflect on assessment outcomes. As teachers gather information from formative assessment, they adjust their instruction to further student learning.

In brief: Formative assessment

- Provides a way to align standards, content, and assessment
- Allows for the purposeful selection of strategies
- Embeds assessment in instruction
- Guides instructional decisions

In practice: During a high school social studies unit on the development of American nationalism after the War of 1812, Mr. Sandusky uses a series of assessments to monitor his students' developing understanding of the presented material. Mr. Sandusky begins with a pre-assessment focused on content similar to what students will encounter in the final selected-response test. After reviewing the pre-assessment data, he concludes that his students either remember little of their prior learning about the material or haven't been exposed to these topics before. He had intended to begin the unit with a discussion of how the popularity of "The Star-Spangled Banner" fueled nationalistic spirit but decides to alter those plans somewhat by having students read articles about the War of 1812, grouping them by readiness and assigning purposefully selected readings. One group reads about the reasons the United States and Britain went to war, another reads about specific events that occurred during the war, and a third reads about Francis Scott Key. Each group reports out, sharing information with the rest of the class.

As the unit progresses, students keep track of their learning and assignments on a work-along, turning it in to Mr. Sandusky every day for a quick check. For example, they describe causes of the war, answer a question about Key's motivation to write "The Star-Spangled Banner," and note the location of the battle he observed (Baltimore's Fort McHenry). This is followed by a Corners activity where students pick different lines of the song to analyze and respond to in terms of relevance to current events. Later, after a discussion of the diverse opinions on the War of 1812, the teacher asks students to report one pro and one con viewpoint. To probe students' understanding of the significant outcomes of the war, he asks the class to describe three specific changes in the power of the U.S. government that resulted from the war. In these activities, Mr. Sandusky works to align his formative assessment questions with the lesson's specific objectives, incorporate the questions into instruction, and use the information to guide future instruction.

Formative Assessment Is Outcomes Based

Formative assessment focuses on achieving goals rather than determining if a goal was or was not met, and one of the ways it does so is by helping to clarify learning goals and standards for both teachers and students. Teaching and learning are based on these standards. Students know the criteria for meeting the standards and are frequently shown exemplars.

Teachers give frequent and substantive feedback to students about their progress, pointing out both strengths and areas that need improvement. Teachers plan steps to move students closer to learning goals. Work is assessed primarily on quality in relation to standards rather than student attitude or effort.

In brief: Formative assessment

- Emphasizes learning outcomes
- Makes goals and standards transparent to students
- Provides clear assessment criteria
- Closes the gap between what students know and desired outcomes
- Provides feedback that is comprehensible, actionable, and relevant
- Provides valuable diagnostic information by generating informative data

In practice: A curricular standard for 10th grade Biology requires that students understand the chemical basis of all living things. In her classroom, Ms. Jefferson asks students to track their progress toward the specific objective of describing, comparing, and contrasting the molecular structure of proteins, carbohydrates, and fats. The applied learning comes from explaining how these differences are exhibited by foods that students eat every day. Ms. Jefferson uses a signaling activity to get a baseline assessment of where her students stand; afterward, she delivers a traditional lecture, beginning the lesson (as she will all lessons) by stating the specific learning outcome students are expected to master and then focusing on transitioning students from what they know to what they need to know. Students keep a record of their learning by recording specific content knowledge in lab report notebooks. In one section, they draw the molecular structure of proteins, carbohydrates, and fats. Later in the unit, they watch a video and fill in a provided empty outline and then complete a lab in which they test a variety of foods for the presence of proteins, carbohydrates, and fats and report their findings in their lab notebooks. Ms. Jefferson reviews these notebooks regularly to monitor student progress and understanding, provide specific feedback, and inform her instructional decisions. Other formative assessment strategies she uses include Bump in the Road and Feathers and Salt.

A Brief History of Formative Assessment

As with most effective teaching methods and practices, individual teachers have probably used formative assessment throughout history. Indeed, we could claim Socrates as an early practitioner. Peppering his students with questions that probed and provoked, he used their responses to measure their learning and guide his instruction; this is the primary attribute of formative assessment.

Although teachers have long used strategies like the Socratic method and other forms of meaningful questioning, the term "formative assessment" is a relatively new one. Its contemporary use is often traced to Michael Scriven (1967), who used "formative" and "summative" to indicate differences in both the goals for collecting evaluation information and how that information is then used. Scriven explained that while a program is in the planning and developmental stages, it is still malleable, and the information gathered from evaluation can therefore contribute to change in the program. He called evaluation for this purpose of improving "formative." Once a program has been created and implemented, Scriven argued, evaluations can only yield information to determine whether the program has met its intended goals. Scriven called this final gathering of information a "summative evaluation."

Benjamin Bloom was one of the first to apply the concepts of formative versus summative to educational assessment, helping to lay the foundations for the concept of mastery learning (Bloom, Hastings, & Madaus, 1971). The purpose of mastery learning was to ensure that students didn't move forward to the next level of learning until they had demonstrated mastery of the learning objectives set for the current level. This concept, in turn, became the basis for modular instruction, widespread in the 1970s, in which students learned from self-directed packets, or modules of instruction. When a student successfully completed one packet, he or she could move on to the next packet, proceeding through modules until all objectives were met. In theory, mastery learning resembles today's scaffolding, but in practice, students worked mostly in isolation without much teacher support or peer interaction.

In the decades following, formative assessment began to be more widely explored. States considered ways to embed it in standardized tests. Bloom continued his theoretical work, examining several issues relating to formative assessment. He identified two essential elements of formative learning: feedback for students and corrective conditions for all important components of learning (Bloom, 1977). He also argued that formative information could be used to divide the class into cooperative groups based on the corrections required. From this point, teachers could differentiate instruction to meet the needs of individual students through selected teaching strategies and corrective responses (Bloom, 1976).

In New Zealand, Terry Crooks studied the effect of classroom assessment practices on students and reported on their potential to emphasize what is important to learn and positively affect student motivation. Crooks (1988) asserted that classroom assessment "appears to be one of the most potent forces influencing education. Accordingly it deserves very careful planning and considerable investment of time from educators" (p. 476). Around the same time, Sadler (1989) reasoned that assessment is most effective when students can monitor the quality of their own work through specific provisions that are incorporated directly into instruction.

Perhaps the biggest step forward in the embrace of formative assessment came in 1998, when Paul Black and Dylan Wiliam completed a meta-analysis of more than 250 research studies on the topic. Their findings, published as "Inside the Black Box," make a compelling case for formative assessment. Black and Wiliam's review concluded that "there is no other way of raising standards for which such a strong prima facie case can be made" (1998, p. 148).

"Inside the Black Box" led the way for many educational leaders to define and apply formative assessment in classrooms, not just in the United States but throughout the world. New Zealand, Australia, and Great Britain have been especially strong leaders in this movement. The recent groundswell in interest and information is creating an imperative to change how we think about and use assessment.

Evidence for Formative Assessment

The 1998 Black and Wiliam study provided evidence that formative assessment can make a difference in learning outcomes at all grade levels. This review of research studies, journal articles, and book excerpts concluded that "formative assessment shows an effect size of between .4 and .7, the equivalent of going from the 50th percentile to the 65th" (p. 141). An effect size is a comparison of a range of scores of students exposed to a specific practice to those of students who were not exposed to the practice. Black and Wiliam drew additional conclusions, each of which is worthy of further research:

- The success of formative assessment is highly related to how teachers use it to adjust teaching and learning practices.
- Effective learning is based on active student involvement.
- Enhanced feedback is crucial to improved outcomes.
- There is a link between formative assessment and self-assessment.

More information about the Black and Wiliam study is available through the Web site of Kings College London (www.kcl.ac.uk/schools/sspp/education/research/groups/assess.html).

At the National Research Council, Bransford, Brown, and Cocking's work *How People Learn* (1999) became the basis for the book *Knowing What Students Know* (Pellegrino, Chudowsky, & Glaser, 2001) and drew the following conclusions:

- An assessment plan must come first, not last, in the educational process.
- Assessment, by necessity, integrates knowledge, skills, procedures, and dispositions.
- Assessment as a diagnosis of student progress shifts the emphasis from summative to formative.

In a follow-up to "Inside the Black Box," Wiliam, Lee, Harrison, and Black (2004) examined the achievement of secondary students in math and science who were exposed and not exposed to formative assessment. Teachers involved in the study were trained and supported in their use of classroom-based formative assessment. The research team measured the effects of formative assessment on learning outcomes and found a mean effect size of 0.32 when exposed to the intervention. Also in 2004, Ruiz-Primo and Furtak measured the effect of three formative assessment strategies—eliciting, recognizing, and using information—in the science classroom. They found that the quality of teachers' formative assessment practices was positively linked to the students' level of learning.

The research base for formative assessment will continue to grow, and we look forward to additional data that can strengthen the case for assessing formatively, help confirm best practices for teachers, and pinpoint the most effective strategies for responding to data and for measuring formative assessment's effect on learning outcomes.

Moving Forward with Formative Assessment

In recent years, recommendations for including high-quality formative assessment as an integral part of a larger and more balanced assessment system has come from many groups and organizations, among them the Joint Committee on Standards for Educational Evaluation (2002) and the National Council on Measurement in Education (1995). Content- and level-specific organizations, such as the National Council of Teachers of Mathematics, the National Science Teachers Association, and the National Middle School Association, have also endorsed formative assessment as a way to advance learning.

Although influential organizations and education thought-leaders have reached a general consensus about the benefits of formative assessment, teacher education and training efforts lag behind. As research has shown, teachers get little training or support in assessment and often turn to their untrained peers for information (Black & Wiliam, 1998; Shepard, 2000; Stiggins, 2001, 2002), and we are left with a gap between what we know is effective assessment practice and how most teachers use assessment in the classroom. This deficit in teacher knowledge and practice was the basis of my own doctoral dissertation, in which I concluded that secondary teachers continue to use traditional summative assessment that infrequently aligns with recommended strategies. Shepard (2000) summed it up well when she quoted this observation by Graue (1993): "Assessment and instruction are often conceived as curiously separate in both time and purpose" (p. 4). The key to high-quality formative assessment is to intertwine the two. What teachers and students need is assessment and instruction that are conceived as a unit, employed as a unit, and applied as a unit.

The most important thing you can take away from this discussion of formative assessment is the understanding that no single principle makes assessment formative. It is through the weaving together of all the principles that high-quality formative assessment arises and the blending of assessment and teaching occurs. For a quick overview of what these components look like woven together, see Figure 1.1, which shows the general flow of formative assessment principles.

FIGURE 1.1	The Cycle of Instruction with Formative Assessment

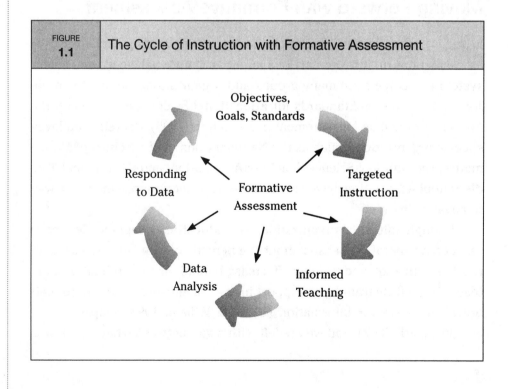

Now let's consider what the cycle of instruction might look like in practice. A teacher preparing for a discussion of current events in an English, social studies, or other class might produce the following plan. (You may not be familiar with some of the plan's strategies, but I will present these in more detail in Part 2 of the book and in the lexicon of strategies in Appendix B.)

Objective, Goal, Standard: Differentiate fact from opinion in written text.
Formative Strategy: Signaling in response to simple sentences read aloud by the teacher.

Targeted Instruction: Identify points of fact as contrasted with expression of the author's opinion in a newspaper editorial.
Formative Strategy: A Corners activity in which the teacher reads more complex sentences and students express their response by going to Fact or Opinion corners. One student in each group presents the group's opinion, and the teacher leads a follow-up discussion.

Informed Teaching: The teacher gives examples of how writers extend fact into opinion along with guidelines for distinguishing fact from opinion. Students read selected text, color-code examples of fact and opinion, and record their responses in their work-alongs.
Formative Strategy: A Think–Pair–Share activity in which students create a color-coded T chart with facts on the left and opinions on the right. This is followed by a whole-class review of the charts to reach consensus.

Data Analysis: The teacher uses data gathered to chart individual and group learning outcomes and target areas of misunderstanding and areas where students need additional challenge.
Formative Strategy: A chart of students' progress, capturing and reflecting on data gathered during Signaling, Corners, the work-along, and the T chart.

Responding to Data: The teacher adjusts instruction and assessment as needed to readdress the objective more effectively.
Formative Strategy: Adjustment to content/resource level of difficulty, grouping students for additional practice or expanded learning, and differentiating the final assessment.

Finding the Balance in Assessment Systems

Large-scale accountability measures have been and will continue to be with us for a long time. The use of formative assessment does not preclude standardized testing but, rather, contributes to a balanced assessment system. Summative assessment has traditionally asked students to definitively express what they know. It's akin to asking, "Are we there yet?" or, "Have we arrived at the intended learning destination?" In comparison, formative assessment asks what route we are taking to reach the goal and in what way the teacher can assist in the journey.

Formative assessment gives teachers continual information on student progress—information that supports decisions about how much and what kind of learning, support, and practice students need to reach the goal. In this model, assessment data come from a variety of activities, rather than from a single assessment at the end. While formative assessment and summative assessment serve the same learning goals, the former is an ongoing process and the latter is a finale: the finish line at the end of the race.

The use of standardized tests alone as the measure of knowledge does not typically lead to improved learning. There is little evidence that standardized tests have raised student achievement except in a few narrow areas, primarily at the elementary level. SAT scores have been generally consistent for many years, and most state standardized test results have flattened out during the past few years. If we want better standardized scores or higher final achievement for our students, we must begin at the classroom level. Research shows that the pathways to school improvement are lined with formative assessment. Students need constructive feedback on how to achieve the targets and guidepost measures along the way, not simply feedback on whether they reached the targets or not. It is formative assessment rather than summative assessment that will make the greatest difference.

As you come to the end of this chapter, please take a moment to consider the questions you may have about the fundamentals of formative assessment. You may want to review any section of this chapter that was not clear to you or move on to Chapter 2, which answers many frequently asked questions about using assessment formatively. Your question may be addressed there.

CHAPTER 2

Questions and Answers About Formative Assessment

Teachers who participate in my workshops often ask very pertinent questions that go right to the heart of formative assessment. I use these questions in a formative manner: to guide my decisions about what to teach and about what material to include in this book. In this chapter, I offer responses to many of those core questions with the hope that in reading them you may find some answers to your own questions about formative assessment.

Is Formative Assessment Something New?

No and yes. The idea of measuring students' progress in learning in order to determine how and what to teach them has been around at least since the time of Socrates. Today's movement to include formative assessment as a routine part of classroom practice, however, has its roots in work spanning the last 40 years.

As noted in Chapter 1, Michael Scriven kicked things off in the late 1960s by coining the term "formative," and others (Bloom, Hastings, & Madaus, 1971; Crooks, 1988; Sadler, 1989) expanded and refined the idea over the next two decades. However, it wasn't until 1998, when Paul Black and Dylan Wiliam published their seminal article "Inside the Black Box: Raising Standards Through Classroom Assessment," that the advancement of formative assessment in today's classrooms and schools began to gain momentum. Black and Wiliam's research led them to the conclusion that formative assessment can raise standards and improve learning outcomes. This evidence moved many educational leaders to define and apply formative assessment in classrooms not just in the United States but worldwide.

How Does Formative Assessment Differ from Other School Reform Efforts?

A teacher once commented that the professional development sessions that kick off every school year always feature the "reform du jour." Over the years, we all have seen many reforms come and go, but formative assessment differs from most in two important ways. First, it incorporates much of what research has told us about how people learn and about best practices for measuring and improving that learning. Second, formative assessment focuses on the day-to-day interactions between the teacher and the students. Teachers routinely using formative assessment in their classroom practice have insight into what and how well their students are learning and know how to quickly adapt instruction to meet students' needs and further progress toward goals. So formative assessment is different in that it is not a reform but a way to *re*form and *in*form education.

Formative assessment's focus on informing instruction also means that it can be used in concert with other educational approaches. Whether you are interested in differentiation, constructivism, authentic learning, or standardized testing, formative assessment can help you help your students along the path to mastery.

What Makes an Assessment Formative?

There are many definitions of formative assessment. Margaret Heritage (2007) describes it as "a systematic process to continuously gather evidence about learning" (p. 140). Carol Boston (2002) explains that it is "the diagnostic use of assessment to provide feedback to teachers and students over the course of instruction" (p. 1). Essentially, formative assessment is a process rather than a product in that it focuses on uncovering what and how well the student understands throughout the course of instruction.

What makes any particular assessment formative is not the specific measuring tool employed but how the information gathered from the tool is used. If a teacher uses information from a particular assessment to track learning, give students feedback, and adjust instructional strategies in a way intended to further progress toward learning goals, that teacher is engaging in formative assessment.

Formative assessment is also a systematic way for teachers and students to gather evidence of learning, engage students in assessment, and use data to improve teaching and learning. When you use an assessment instrument—a test, a quiz, an essay, or any other kind of classroom activity—analytically and diagnostically to measure the process of learning and then, in turn, to inform yourself or your students of progress and guide further learning, you are engaging in formative assessment. If you were to use the same instrument for the sole purpose of gathering data to report to a district or state or to determine a final grade, you would be engaging in summative assessment.

Does Formative Assessment Work in All Content Areas?

Yes, formative assessment is effective for any content area. It can be used in language arts, social studies, science, and math, and it is equally effective in health and PE, the arts, and vocational subjects. It also has potential as an interdisciplinary tool. For example, a pre-assessment asking biology students to summarize what they already know about cell structure yields information about vocabulary as well as content knowledge; the teacher can use this insight to inform instruction in both areas.

How Can Formative Assessment Support the Curriculum?

Curriculum defines the content and sequence of instruction. It identifies the process and products of teaching and learning. Some curricula are broadly designed—think of a scope and sequence or a curriculum map. Other curricula include daily objectives, specific content, learning activities, and assessment strategies.

Formative assessment can support all kinds of curricula by providing essential feedback about what students are learning and how well they are learning it. Formative assessment includes strategies that each teacher can employ on a regular basis in the classroom to track learning. Teachers can then change the content and products of instruction to customize learning based on a student's achievement of curricular goals. In this respect, formative assessment guides curriculum through a reflective process focused on student attainment of the goals and standards.

How Can Formative Assessment Be Used to Establish Instructional Priorities?

Through the consistent use of formative assessment, teachers can quickly gather data to determine whether students are mastering the goals and standards or there are gaps in students' learning. Teachers can then use this information to establish priorities for future lessons. For example, if the majority of your class has mastered a specific standard, you may choose to use instruction time to delve into that standard further or explore an applied aspect of it. If, however, formative assessment data indicate that your students need more instruction or more practice, then you may decide to reteach certain elements or assign more group exercises targeting a particular skill. In this way, formative assessment guides the establishment of priorities for teaching and learning.

Although "data-driven instruction" has become a current buzz phrase, it can mean many different things. Some districts are disaggregating the data from standardized tests and using those data to pinpoint students' strengths and weaknesses. Other districts are using this same information to develop "common formative assessments"—assessments given to students in the same grade and taking the same subject—in order to measure subsets of standardized tests. These strategies have a documented purpose but differ from daily formative assessment in that the teacher cannot immediately and routinely use them to determine teaching priorities.

How Can Formative Assessment Be Used as a Teaching Strategy?

As the saying goes, formative assessment is assessment *for* learning more than it is assessment *of* learning. In a formative assessment classroom, teachers still present information through lecture and demonstration and still set tasks; students still complete these tasks and interact with the teacher and with one another.

There are a variety of specific strategies associated with formative assessment that are designed to gather data related to student understanding and further instructional objectives. The lexicon in Appendix B describes many of these strategies, and the chapters in Part 2 of this book, covering applications of formative assessment before, during, and after instruction, provide specific examples. The most important idea to keep in mind, however, is that formative assessment as a whole is a planned strategy carried out to improve learning.

How Is Formative Assessment Used in Grading?

The answer to this question depends on the teacher. There is a brewing controversy about using formative assessment in grading, and it centers on whether or not to grade all students consistently *at* their level of achievement or to grade their growth *toward* mastery of standards. If a top student arrives knowing about 90 percent of the content and rises to

100-percent mastery during the course (a net gain of 10 percent), should that student receive a higher grade than a student who came in knowing 50 percent of the content and rose to 75-percent mastery (a net gain of 25 percent)? If the expectation is that all students will master certain standards, then grading at the level of achievement will typically reflect the spread of abilities students bring to the class combined with the additional learning they acquire. If we grade progress toward standards, then a student coming in at 50 percent and rising to 75 percent has learned more than the one going from 90 to 100 percent, and therefore, grades will reflect their growth *and* final achievement level rather than just their final achievement level.

Teachers who believe that grading should reflect growth toward standards include selected formative assessment data in grade determination. They typically do not count every formative activity toward a grade but may factor in data used as benchmarks during instruction. The value placed on formative assessment data will vary among teachers, but generally it is weighted less than summative assessment data. Keep in mind that counting some formative assessment data in grading helps to fairly reflect the learning of those students who have difficulty with more traditional testing formats or experience test anxiety. For the purist who believes that grades should reflect only final summative assessments, the compromise is to report that final grade along with improvement indicators. The bottom line is that everything should be assessed, but not everything needs to be graded, and grades should reflect progress and results.

Can Formative Assessment Close Achievement Gaps?

Formative assessment definitely helps to close the gap between what students know and what we want them to know. It makes both teachers and students aware of holes in knowledge or understanding, leading teachers to address specific content and provide additional learning strategies to fill in these holes, leading students to set goals and track their progress toward achieving them. In some states and districts, "closing the gap" means teaching specific test content. In others, teaching students how to think and learn across a broad curriculum is thought more effective. What-ever system you may be operating under, formative assessment can help you close achievement gaps.

What's the Relationship Between Rubrics and Formative Assessment?

Rubrics and formative assessment perform some of the same functions. When used in the formative classroom, rubrics help teachers monitor learning and instruction and also provide meaningful feedback to students. Analytical rubrics include defined criteria that reflect standards, and they have descriptions of varying levels of "quality" performance. When rubrics are given to students prior to an assignment, they help to clarify students' understanding of expectations. Teachers can adapt or adjust a rubric to give more weight to particular criteria in order to differentiate the assign-ment to meet individual needs. Rubrics support revisions of student work because they make it easy for students and teachers to identify changes that need to be made to meet goals. Teachers find that rubrics make assess-ment more objective because work is rated only on the given criteria. The development of quality rubrics does take time and thought, but in the long run, they make assessment more consistent and efficient, and the same one can be used for both formative and summative purposes.

How Can I Help My Students Understand Formative Assessment?

Formative assessment can be a revelation to students who have come to think of themselves as "dumb" or as academic losers, because it gives them a clearer idea of what they need to do to succeed: master *this* mate-rial, acquire *this* knowledge, or develop *these* skills. The point of formative assessment is to inform and improve, not to pass judgment. Success breeds success, and motivation grows from it.

Use formative assessment from the first day of class, and be sure you scaffold to catch the students who need more support. Research shows that formative assessment is most effective with students at the lower end of the achievement spectrum. This is not to say that these students are less capable; sometimes, they are just disenfranchised and disconnected from traditional school subjects, and the feedback from formative assessment helps to reengage them.

Do I Have to Do This?

The list of things that teachers have to do is a long one, stretching beyond simply teaching, testing, and reporting grades to engaging parents in their child's learning, participating in professional learning communities (PLCs), and responding to psychosocial dilemmas. But I trust that incorporating formative assessment is something that you are going to *want* to do. Formative assessment is one of the few proven strategies that directly support high-quality instruction and effective assessment. We all want our students to be successful; after all, that is why we become teachers. Teachers incorporate formative assessment because it improves teaching and learning. Try it and you'll see.

How Can I Learn More?

As a starting point for learning more about formative assessment, please consult the References section at the back of the book. Particularly indispensable are the works of Paul Black and Dylan Wiliam (1998), Linda Darling-Hammond (2004), Robert Marzano (2003, 2006), Lori Shepard (2000), Margaret Heritage (2007), W. James Popham (2008), Rick Stiggins (2001, 2002), and Susan Brookhart (1997, 2003).

Teachers know that learning gets embedded when it is observed, practiced, discussed, and taught to others. After you have read this book and other source materials, I hope you will reflect on what you have learned. Discuss formative assessment with others. Start a study group or add discussion to PLC time. Attend a workshop or a class. Apply your new knowledge in the classroom.

PART 2

Using
Formative Assessment

- How can a teacher best balance pre-planned assessment strategies with on-the-spot formative assessment?
- How can pre-assessment be designed to measure not only knowledge but also attitudes and beliefs?
- What can a teacher do when a seemingly well-designed unit of instruction falls flat?
- How should a teacher respond when gaps in student skills and knowledge become apparent when the class is well into a lesson?
- How can teachers know when and where to use formative assessment during instruction? Are some places or times better than others?
- Are certain formative assessment strategies better suited to particular content areas?
- What is formative assessment's role in determining students' readiness for summative assessment?

Your turn: Take a quick scan of the chapters in this section and write two other questions that immediately come to mind.

Evidence that formative assessment improves teaching and learning continues to grow. The first part of the book laid a foundation for understanding why formative assessment works. In this part, we will look at when and how to use it effectively in the classroom.

Chapters 3, 4, and 5 present many tools and strategies for diagnosing students' learning needs before, during, and after instruction and offer many options for responding to those needs. In-depth explanations of how to use each tool or strategy are followed by examples of classroom practice. We will also meet many middle and high school teachers who are working diligently to use formative assessment to improve learning outcomes in their classrooms. Their classes span just about every content area, so whether you teach social studies, science, math, English, the arts, health, or vocational subjects, you will encounter examples that are relevant to your work.

Keep in mind that formative assessment is not an additional instructional activity to be added on to what a teacher does but, rather, a planned process that aligns with standards, goals, and objectives and proceeds in a logical sequence. When you use assessment consistently throughout instruction, it will help you move students from basic knowledge to deeper understanding and from knowledge and understanding to the higher cognitive levels of synthesis, analysis, and application. In these chapters, we will look at how to use assessment in a selective, intentional, and deliberate way to shift the focus to the student and the priority to learning outcomes. You will discover how to apply gathered assessment data to your teaching, targeting instruction to specific identified goals and standards. And you will learn to design and plan assessment and instruction so that they work hand in hand to support student learning.

A curriculum director once asked me whether a workshop on classroom assessment strategies would really offer her teachers anything new. I explained that for the most part, teachers do not have much in-depth knowledge about assessment because teacher education and professional development programs do not make it a priority. The result is that teachers are hungry for information about assessment, and, in my workshops, they routinely ask for examples of formative assessment that are specific to their subject and grade. I always give them an opportunity to select a strategy I have presented, work with other teachers, and develop ways to customize and personalize it for their own content area, grade level, and students.

My aim in this part of the book is to provide that same opportunity. As you read through the next three chapters, stop, reflect, and apply the ideas discussed to your own circumstances. I've also included case studies at the end of each chapter. These are examples of practice that show a range of teacher expertise in assessing, and I invite you to analyze the case, decide if the teacher has used assessment formatively, and identify ways in which the teacher could improve practice. You can then compare your ideas to the analysis I provide.

CHAPTER 3

Formative Assessment Prior to Instruction

How does a teacher plan more effective instruction? In *The 7 Habits of Highly Effective People*, Stephen Covey (1989) explains the benefits of putting first things first: to allow us to focus on the important outcome and then devise the steps necessary to get there. This practice is equally beneficial in the classroom. Rather than habitually following a prescribed lesson plan, teachers need to focus on the learning outcomes we intend our students to achieve and use these goals to drive instruction. Pre-assessment is the means we use to chart the initial course.

The Power of Pre-assessment

Pre-assessment is a routine part of most people's jobs. Before ordering inventory, a store owner will first find out what items have been selling and how well. Car mechanics perform diagnostics on an engine before trying to fix that funny noise it's making. Dentists take X-rays to assess teeth before deciding to drill. And doctors check blood pressure, pulse, and weight and ask a slew of questions before deciding what action to take with a patient. Yet teachers frequently begin instruction without performing any kind of pre-assessment of their students' knowledge or skills.

Teachers need information to make accurate diagnoses and prescriptions for learning. Finding out what students know before beginning instruction allows teachers to focus teaching on what students haven't yet learned, avoiding redundancy. Pre-assessment results can also guide teachers in determining the level of challenge and difficulty each student needs and what the final individual learning targets should be. Customizing instruction makes it more relevant, engaging, and motivational for the individual learner. Pre-assessment is key to effective instructional design, and it is the first and most crucial step in using formative assessment. After all, how can we measure growth in learning without knowing the starting point? Let's examine some specific uses and benefits of formative assessment conducted prior to instruction.

Clarification of Prior Knowledge and Skills

A pre-assessment of knowledge and skills can be formal or informal. Pre-tests, a more formal measure, have been around for a long time and can be used to quickly determine a student's background knowledge. For example, if I were teaching a class on the content of this chapter, I might use a binary-choice pretest that looks like this:

Mark each statement as true or false.

1. I feel confident in my ability to measure students' knowledge, skills, and attitudes at the beginning of a unit of instruction.   T   F
2. I know of at least three strategies for pre-assessing students' knowledge, skills, and dispositions.   T   F
3. Once I have pre-assessed my students, I am able to use that information in my instructional practices.   T   F

A Likert-style scale format would also be appropriate.

In the lesson following this pre-test, I would use the information gleaned to adjust my instructional design and content. If most students self-reported that they were knowledgeable and confident about the pre-assessment process, I would focus on extending and deepening their basic knowledge, and I would purposefully incorporate formative assessment throughout instruction. If the pre-test indicated students had limited understanding of pre-assessment, then I would begin by focusing on foundational knowledge and formatively measure students' understanding before asking them to apply their knowledge, use it in higher-level thinking, or take a summative test.

Let's consider some other examples of pre-testing. Mr. Nelson, in his high school civics class, uses a pre-assessment to determine his students' knowledge of the Bill of Rights. Before he begins teaching this unit, he wants to find out how many of the rights they know and what they understand about them. Mr. Nelson's civics pre-test looks like this:

1. Which of these foundational documents of American history came first?
   a. The Constitution
   b. The Declaration of Independence
   c. The Bill of Rights
2. Which one of these is not in the Bill of Rights?
   a. Freedom of religion
   b. The right to bear arms
   c. The pursuit of happiness
3. If you could have only three rights in the Bill of Rights, which would you choose and why?

Mrs. Peterson uses pre-testing in her middle school two-dimensional art class. Before she starts a unit on art history, she distributes the following pre-assessment:

1. Name three famous painters and their style of work, such as abstract, Impressionist, or pop art.
2. What are three factors that influence an artist's work?
3. Select one of the painters you listed and explain what you know about their time period, style, and medium.
4. Describe the differences between watercolor, acrylic, and oil paints.

Both Mr. Nelson and Mrs. Peterson can use the data these tests generate to decide how to adjust the content and depth of their instruction and to set individual and class learning goals. Later in the chapter, I'll discuss other pre-assessment strategies that can provide similar snapshots of prior knowledge and skills.

Insight into the Depth of Prior Knowledge

In addition to showing the breadth of what students know, pre-assessments can be designed to reveal students' depth of understanding, which is an important piece of information to have when designing instruction. Look, for example, at the third question of Mr. Nelson's civics pre-assessment, asking students which three rights they would choose to have and why. It is set up to tell Mr. Nelson not only *if* students can name three rights beyond the two listed in question #2 but also how well they understand why those rights were formally enshrined. In this case, he learns that while all 16 of his students could name the 3 rights they valued most, only 5 were able to expand on their choices with well-thought-out reasons. He interprets the data to mean that his students have good baseline knowledge of the Bill of Rights and he ought to focus his instruction on comprehension, application, and analysis.

Here are some other questions Mr. Nelson might use on a pre-assessment to gain insight into the depth of students' prior knowledge and help him decide how best to structure his unit:

1. Under the First Amendment, which of the following are allowed, and why? A newspaper article describing charges of mayoral breach of ethics; publically calling the principal a liar; a Facebook update stating that a friend is "a slut."
2. Which First Amendment right do the following actions proceed from? Holding an anti-war protest in front of the White House; a town's decision to set up a Nativity scene in front of Town Hall but not a menorah; police officers needing a search warrant before entering a person's home.
3. Review a series of newspaper articles and identify instances of First Amendment rights being protected or abused.
4. Describe a world without one of the rights now enshrined in the First Amendment.

Identification of Predispositions, Values, and Beliefs

Students have different backgrounds and experiences that influence learning. Some have fixed beliefs that may affect how they receive instruction. For instance, students who have been exposed only to creationism may be confused by or resistant to instruction on evolution. Similarly, students who have experienced a traumatic family event may bring a different perspective to novels such as *The Memory Keeper's Daughter* or *The Secret Life of Bees.*

Identifying students' predispositions, values, and beliefs, however, requires a different type of pre-assessment than a pre-test designed to measure knowledge and skills. To elicit these less quantifiable and more sensitive pieces of information, employ open-ended questioning techniques that invite students to express their ideas. For example, prior to asking students to read a novel that features the effects of divorce on a teenager, an English teacher could ask students to complete an open-ended sentence such as, "Some of the ways that divorce affects people's lives include _____." Or a teacher might give students a fill-in-the-blank question to reveal differences between values at home and at school: "It's easy to get confused between what is taught at school about (_____) and what I have learned about this topic at home." For some students, a pre-assessment that asks them to draw a picture of or otherwise illustrate their ideas about a more sensitive subject can provide illumination to both teacher and student.

Identification of Prior Learning Sources

Knowing where students got the information they currently possess about an upcoming topic of instruction can help ensure effective instruction designed to address and correct misinformation that could derail learning. The Internet and social networking, for example, have become primary resources for students, and the reliability of some online sources is certainly up for debate. A teacher who discovers that students rely heavily on less trustworthy sources might make effective research practices a specific point of instruction. Consider the example of Mr. Fey. While explaining to a class that Wikipedia and blogs are not acceptable resources, he spontaneously asks his students where else they might look for information online. A few students researching breakfast cereals mention that they are using a cereal company's Web site as the source for claiming that a certain cereal (one with a high proportion of brightly colored marshmallows) is a good source of fiber and antioxidants. This comment prompts Mr. Fey to circle back and launch a mini-lesson on "search savvy": how to look at source, content, and accuracy in an objective manner. Notice that this pre-assessment was not planned and that the teacher uses the data that emerge from it to make an on-the-spot instructional response.

Guidance on Goal Pursuit and Attainment

Pre-assessment can provide a common guide for pursuing and reaching goals. With her students about to embark on a long-term research project, Miss Morris maps out each stage of the project into parts. Her intent is to incorporate reference and citation skills into the project from the start, and she explains to students that each of them will be compiling an annotated bibliography of their sources. She explains how to go about this and shares exemplars. As students work on their projects over the next two weeks, Miss Morris checks in on the bibliographies taking shape. Those who are struggling with the process and product work with Miss Morris to learn more about bibliographies, identify resources, and practice their skill in describing sources.

Cognitive Preparation for Learning

Cognitively, formative pre-assessments have several advantages. Brain research shows that the activation of prior knowledge promotes the brain's ability to make connections to new learning and improve comprehension. It is the brain's natural mechanism to try to fit new learning into existing knowledge. Besides calling up prior learning, pre-assessment can also encourage reflection, which supports the organization of thinking and extension of understanding. Additionally, emerging research on memory shows that information is best remembered when it is actively or emotionally processed. Many of the informal pre-assessment strategies I'll present promote this kind of student engagement. The strategies also help teachers to get students' attention, which, according to Eric Jensen (2000), is important at the beginning of teaching and pre-assessments.

REMEMBER

Use formative asssessment prior to instruction to

- Determine student's incoming knowledge and skill levels
- Reveal students' depth of knowledge
- Illuminate students' incoming attitudes, dispositions, and beliefs
- Identify sources of incoming information
- Guide student and teacher planning
- Clarify the gap between current and desired achievement levels
- Prepare students' brains for learning

Strategies and Tools for Assessing Prior to Instruction

There is a wide variety of innovative and engaging strategies and tools that support formative pre-assessment. I have chosen four especially effective and versatile ones to highlight here: *Entrance Slips, Corners, Gallery,* and *sticky notes*. Additional strategies, with brief explanations, are provided in Appendix B.

I encourage you to experiment to see which approaches work best for you and your students. Every class and every teacher is unique, and what works in one classroom or subject may not work in another. You'll discover that the strategies are flexible and that one may lend itself to different applications at different points in instruction. For example, some pre-assessments may also be used formatively during or even after instruction.

It's important to keep in mind that these early formative assessment activities are most effective when they are ungraded, brief, nonthreatening, connected to content and standards, and targeted toward instructional improvement. The goal of pre-assessment is to gather information, not intimidate students or embarrass them. In the pages to come, I provide some hints for making the strategies feel less threatening, and some of these strategies have these characteristics built in.

Entrance Slips

An entrance slip is a student's response to a question a teacher poses related to the upcoming instruction. For example, a teacher might ask, "What's the relationship between *A* and *B*?" or, "What do you find confusing about *C*?" and then ask students to write their answer on a piece of paper. An Entrance Slip activity should take only a few minutes at the beginning of a period of instruction. Teachers can ask students to sign the slips or to submit them anonymously (or with randomly assigned numbers), if responses are to be publicly posted or discussed as a way to ease into the topic and gain further information about prior knowledge. Especially when shared, entrance slips can pique students' interest and, at the same time, give teachers feedback on students' current levels of understanding, their higher-level thinking skills, or their personal beliefs. As we know, this is critical information for differentiating and customizing instruction.

I like to hang on to entrance slips and return them to students at the conclusion of the unit of instruction. At that point, they serve as a measure of learning and help students to self-assess and reflect the achievement they've made.

In practice: Before beginning a unit on presidential elections one year, Mr. Walker asks students in his civics class to submit an entrance slip response to a question about how the president is elected:

Which of the following is true?

_____ Presidents are elected by a majority vote of the people.

_____ Presidents are elected by a group of selected representatives.

Pick one:

_____ Each state has two members of the Electoral College.

_____ Each state has the same number of Electoral College members as it has members of the House of Representatives in Washington, D.C.

When Mr. Walker collects the slips, he finds that most students believe that the president is chosen by the popular vote alone. In response to this information, he decides to devote more instructional time to the basics of the election process.

During the following year, a presidential election year, the election process is much discussed in the media. When Mr. Walker uses an Entrance Slip activity to find out what the new group of students knows about presidential elections, he finds that most of them are familiar with the popular vote and know about the Electoral College. Mr. Walker adjusts his instructional plans accordingly. After a relatively brief review of the election process, he moves on to an application-focused activity, giving students the choice of writing to Congress to share their thoughts about the election system or staging their own mock election with popular and delegate voting.

Teachers can also use this strategy to gather information about students' belief systems. For example, before Ms. Marsh assigns her English students *The Kite Runner*, she asks them to complete the following entrance slip:

1. What are three words that come to mind when you think of Afghanistan?
2. How would you describe the relationship between betrayal and forgiveness?

The first question is a way to begin uncovering students' prior knowledge and predispositions about Afghanistan's history and culture. Ms. March asks about students' understanding of betrayal and forgiveness so that she can get a better idea of the values, belief systems, or possible stereotypes they will bring to the reading of the book.

Based on the data collected through these slips, she decides on a follow-up activity that will focus her students' attention on the lives of Afghani people. First, she posts pieces of paper on which she's printed "Media Images of Afghanistan," "Human Rights in Afghanistan," and "History of Afghanistan." Then, she asks students to move throughout the room and list on these pieces of paper things they know or believe to be true about the topic. Their responses suggest to Ms. March that the media has had a powerful effect on students' ideas about Afghanistan and that many of them think of it mostly as "a country of terrorists." She decides that before her students read *The Kite Runner,* they'd benefit from a more nuanced perspective, and so she arranges to bring in a guest speaker who lived in Afghanistan for many years. This, she hopes, will help open the eyes of students who have a very narrow view of the country. She also believes the guest speaker will be interesting to the handful of students who have a bit more background knowledge of the topic and increase their engagement with the novel.

At the start of his health unit on obesity, Mr. Gianni uses the Entrance Slip strategy to find out what students might know or want to know about the topic. He encourages students to ask questions based on what they have heard at home or in the media. Asking students to pose their own questions is an especially relevant strategy for topics that have high visibility in the media and about which the media may give out both powerful messages and incorrect information. Mr. Gianni's pre-assessment looks like this:

> List three causes of obesity, and write a question you have about each cause. Here are some hints: consider genetics, lifestyle, exercise, food choices, etc. Sample question: *Why do my sister and I eat almost the exact same foods, but our weights are very different?*

Based on the entrance slips, Mr. Gianni finds that his students have different levels of knowledge about obesity and that he'll need to cover both general information and more advanced material for students who already have a good baseline understanding of the topic. He opens the unit with a PowerPoint overview of the topic and then divides students into two groups based on the accuracy of their understanding of obesity. To students who still need more fundamental understanding, he assigns a vocabulary-building exercise focusing on terms essential for understanding, such as *metabolism* and *BMI.* Students who showed more depth in their understanding he asks to debate the question of who bears the responsibility for obesity: the individual, the family, the media, or corporations. He also asks this group to compile a list prioritizing these groups from most to least responsible based on their discussion. This example illustrates how entrance slips can help a teacher differentiate assignments.

Here are some sample Entrance Slip questions for a range of content areas. How might the responses they generate contribute to the teacher's understanding of students' knowledge and skills? Their attitudes and beliefs? How might a teacher use the resulting data to inform instructional plans?

- *Math:* What does slope measure, and where is it used in real life?
- *English:* What do you think the protagonist will do next?
- *Science:* Our last class focused on the causes of global warming. What part of our last discussion did you understand *most*? What part did you understand *least*?
- *Spanish:* What do you know about Cinco de Mayo?
- *Art:* Which Impressionist painter do you like best, and why: Cezanne, Renoir, or Monet?
- *Interdisciplinary:* If the ocean levels rose 10 feet today, how would your life change?

Your turn: Think about your own classroom and how you might frame and use an entrance slip for a particular unit of study.

Corners

Corners gives teachers a quick and visual way to preview what their students may know or believe before instruction begins. For this strategy, the teacher chooses a question that reflects the content of the upcoming instruction and labels corners of the room with possible answers, one answer per corner. The teacher then asks the students the question and tells them to go to the corner with the label that best matches their answer. As the teacher takes note of where the students go, the members of the group collaboratively record statements or arguments to support this point of view or belief. These are additional data that the teacher can examine and consider when designing the upcoming lesson.

Because student answers are more public in this pre-assessment strategy than entrance slips, teachers need to be sensitive to individual students who may be less comfortable making a public statement. Collecting individual written notes and votes in a corner can address this concern. Instead of asking students to stand in a corner, teachers can ask them to sign their name at a selected corner or write a response on a posted paper in the corner.

Corners also can serve as an assessment at other points in instruction, but as a pre-assessment it gives both teachers and students useful information. Teachers get individual and whole-class baseline measures of student knowledge and dispositions. As the students work together to support their corner "choice," teachers can gather information about students' higher-order and critical/evaluative thinking on a topic. For students, the Corners strategy prompts them to reflect on what they know or believe about a topic and, when prompted, to supply supporting evidence and evaluate the accuracy of that knowledge or opinion.

Please note that Corners can be adapted to any number of possible answers to a question. You can use two corners for two-sided issues, such as whether or not cell phone use should be allowed in school, whether or not cloning is ethical, or whether ethanol is good or bad for the environment. You can also expand the strategy to four corners to accommodate questions with four possible answers: Which of the four primary candidates would you choose for president? You could even make corner labels that reflect levels of agreement with a statement, like a Likert-style scale, so students can place themselves on a continuum of possible answers.

In practice: At the beginning of a unit of study on global warming, Mrs. Jones tapes long sheets of newsprint paper in the four corners of her classroom. She writes a different heading on each sheet—"Automobiles," "Deforestation," "Manufacturing Plants," and "Nonhuman Factors"—and then launches the activity by asking students to go to the corner of the room labeled with what they think is the biggest contributor to global warming. There, they are to generate a list of what they know about the problem. After a five-minute brainstorming period, each group shares its list with the rest of the class. The distribution of her students in the room's four corners indicates to Mrs. Jones that her students see global warming as equally attributable to human and nonhuman factors; however, the groups of students reporting out on human factors are expressing themselves with a great deal of passion, and the entire class is listening intently. Mrs. Jones decides to build on this engagement and begin her instruction with a look at the human causes of global warming.

This type of foundational assessment can also point the way to numerous instructional strategies that a teacher may use, such as a PowerPoint lecture, an Internet research project to check the accuracy of the statements generated by the group, or a group or individual research project on specific facts, truths, and essential understandings of the topic.

Ms. Gough also uses Corners to pre-assess her psychology students. She labels three corners in her room as "Agree," "Disagree," and "Unsure." She then asks her psychology students to go to the corner that best matches their response to statements about parenting, which she reads aloud. These include assertions such as "Spanking is an effective way of disciplining children" and "Women are better than men at child rearing." After the students go to their selected corners, they discuss among themselves their reasons for going there. Ms. Gough then asks the members of each group to explain to the other groups why they selected their corner. Listening to these reports, Ms. Gough learns that almost all of her students view spanking as ineffective, and she makes a note to minimize formal lecture on this topic. Instead, she'll simply reinforce this belief by showing a brief video focused on alternative discipline strategies. She also learns that the majority of the class believes women are better at parenting than men and makes a note to emphasize issues of gender and parenting in her upcoming instruction.

As an introduction to a lesson on ethics, Mr. Wilson uses masking tape to create a line across the width of the classroom and asks students to place themselves on the continuum in a manner that reflects their degree of agreement with the statement "Lying is OK." Standing at the far left of the line, he explains, is how they should indicate "I think lying is never OK." The farther along the line students place themselves, the greater their agreement that lying is an acceptable behavior. Then Mr. Wilson asks the students to reorder themselves on the line to show the amount of lying that they regularly engage in. A discussion ensues on what is a lie, why people lie, and when, if ever, lying is acceptable. Noting where his students position themselves and listening to their comments, Mr. Wilson concludes that most of them are at the early level of the conventional state of Kohlberg's moral development. The topic lends itself to a social-learning approach, and Mr. Wilson decides to incorporate discussion of case studies into his upcoming lessons in order to move students along to a deeper understanding of conventional reasoning and post conventional thinking. Afterward, he'll have the class review and discuss a research study reporting that although most students admit to cheating in school, most students also believe cheating is wrong.

REFLECT AND APPLY

Here are some sample questions from different content areas that would work well with the Corners strategy. How might the responses they generate contribute to the teacher's understanding of students' knowledge and skills? Their attitudes and beliefs? How might teachers use the data generated to inform instructional decisions?

- *Math:* Should the United States use the metric or English system of measurement?
- *World Language:* Which language should be the second language of the United States: Spanish, French, Chinese, or something else?
- *Language Arts:* Do you prefer to access a book through written, audio, or video versions?
- *Career Choices:* What is most important to you: money, personal satisfaction, getting recognition, or being the best?

Your turn: Think about your own classroom and the units of study you teach. How might you use Corners as a pre-assessment strategy?

Gallery

When used as a pre-assessment, the Gallery method, like Corners, gives teachers and students a visual picture of student knowledge and skills or viewpoints. The idea of this strategy is to make a display, or gallery, of student responses to a teacher-generated question. All forms of responses can be considered here: images, computer graphics, single words or phrases, drawings, and so on. Sometimes Gallery is called Graffiti Wall; this name conveys the self-expression that this strategy can encourage as well as its typical logistics: having students record their response on a common sheet of paper. However, don't let the self-expressive association discourage you from using Gallery in a class that's usually not associated with self-expression. It is just as applicable in a statistics or physics class as it is in a fine arts or language arts class. Gallery can be used to capture student knowledge of everything from math problems to multicultural issues.

As with other types of pre-assessments, Gallery submissions can be posted with the creator's name, posted with a code number that identifies the creator to the teacher but not to other students, or posted anonymously. Names or codes provide data for subsequent grouping; anonymous responses are well-suited for whole-class discussion of the gallery, an approach that gives everyone the opportunity to work collaboratively toward an understanding of the material. Anonymous submissions are a particularly good idea when the material or topic is new and it's likely that most students will have limited background knowledge.

In practice: To start a unit about graphs and charts, Mrs. Zakari posts one problem and asks students to solve it on a piece of paper, which she will collect and review. Mrs. Zakari knows that her students have encountered graphs and charts in past instruction. Her plan is to go more deeply into design and creation. She also wants students to understand why particular chart or graph formats are suited to particular data sets. So she begins with a question that she believes most students will answer easily: *Where have you seen charts and graphs used in the real world?*

Mrs. Zakari collects students' anonymous responses and quickly sorts them into categories (e.g., "in the newspaper," "at school"). Then, being clear that there will be no grade involved, she asks students to draw one of these charts or graphs they have seen as accurately as possible. They respond with all kinds of illustrations, taping them to the class whiteboard and then participating in a whole-class brainstorming session focused on the various data that could be gathered about them and their school and how those data could be communicated. The knowledge her students display tells Mrs. Zakari that most of them know about pie charts and bar graphs but are less clear on why or when to use them. She will use this pre-assessment information to plan a strategy for the upcoming unit.

To make a Gallery activity more engaging and interesting, teachers can decorate the paper or wall where students post their work. They can make the area look like graph paper, a forest of trees, or another image that relates to the topic. For example, at the start of a sociology unit on understanding cultural similarities and differences and the wide range of factors that influence cultures, Mr. Velez gives each of his students a piece of paper that looks like a brick. He asks students to share a belief, icon, or ritual from their own or another culture by writing it on their "brick." Students put their names on the back of their bricks, and he collects and reviews the submissions—to gain insight and ensure appropriateness—before posting them on the wall. Together, the class builds a multicultural graffiti wall, and students do a walk-through to review all the postings. Just in that tour of their wall, students learn a great deal about cultural variation.

Following their tour, Mr. Velez encourages students to ask questions about things they want to learn more about. The discussion leads to a K-W-L activity, during which Mr. Velez makes discreet notes about topics that seem to interest his students and about which of his students know about specific cultures. The former information he can use to sharpen his instructional plans and provide interest-based hooks; the latter information he can file away and use to elicit comments whenever a discussion of particular cultures comes up or when he wants to set up small groups with a heterogeneous or homogeneous cultural perspective. As the activity continues, Mr. Velez also concludes that the members of this class know a great deal about their own cultures and little about the cultures of others, but they are curious to learn more. This positive attitude is encouraging.

Here's another example of the Gallery strategy in practice. Miss Agosta, a new English teacher, keeps trying new ways to get her students excited about reading novels. She knows they have read lots of fiction over the years but have sometimes struggled to relate to the characters or engage in the plot. She decides to try a Gallery display.

Her first step is a Quickdraw activity. She asks the students to graphically illustrate their favorite novels, sign their names, and post their illustrations. Miss Agosta takes note of the various genres of these favorite novels and uses this information to quickly separate the students into interest-based groups: science fiction, mystery/thrillers, romance, historical novels, and so on. Next, each group summarizes their genre's key elements: its general approach to plot, place/setting, characters, and conflict. While they are working, Miss Agosta posts four pieces of chart paper throughout the room, each headed with one of the four key elements: "Plot," "Place/Setting," "Characters," and "Conflict." At her signal, group members move about the room, adding relevant characteristics of their genre under these element headings.

The International Reading Association has a standard that requires students to create an original story based on synthesis of other novels. This Gallery display provides the foundation for each group to create as far-fetched and improbable a story as they could, while still clearly showing the four elements. Here, the strategy of starting with an individual display of a novel illustration and following with a summary and identification of elements shows how a pre-assessment can blossom into an ongoing process of assessment for learning.

REFLECT AND APPLY

Gallery is typically a fun and engaging pre-assessment. Here is a list of ways teachers in different content areas might use this strategy. How might the responses they generate contribute to the teacher's understanding of students' knowledge and skills? Their attitudes and beliefs? What kind of information would each of these generate? How might it inform instruction?

- *Literature:* Write all the vocabulary you know that relates to or describes poetry on paper cut into leaf shapes. Extend this by adding words (leaves to the tree) as the poetry unit progresses.
- *Math:* Illustrate uses of right angles in the real world.
- *Marketing:* List the best and worst ads you have seen. Follow up by analyzing why.
- *Art:* Critique the modern artists Salvador Dali, Andy Warhol, Jackson Pollock, and Piet Mondrian. Next to a painting by each, note your thoughts.

Your turn: Think about your own classroom and how you might frame a question to generate a Gallery display related to a particular unit of study. What would students' responses tell you about their prior learning, skill levels, and beliefs?

■ ■ ■

Sticky Notes

Sticky notes support a variety of assessment techniques involving signaling, sorting, and analysis. Students can use these slips of paper to communicate their starting knowledge and understanding, data teachers can then use to engage students in a lesson or to revise upcoming instructional plans, adding review activities, changing content, adjusting pacing, and so on. Sticky notes are also a great tool for uncovering students' analytical abilities. And because the use of sticky notes often involves movement, these activities are a good option for kinesthetic learners.

In practice: Let's take a look at four strategic ways to use sticky notes: for signaling, for sorting, for engagement, and for analysis.

For signaling. Teachers can put a red and a green sticky note back to back and give one of these two-sided notes to each student. After the teacher introduces a new concept, students can hold up the note with either the green side or the red facing the teacher to indicate whether they know something about the topic or not. Based on these responses, the teacher can move forward with instruction or decide to spend more time on the concept until more students achieve the desired level of mastery. (As we'll discuss further in Chapter 4's look at formative assessment during instruction, teachers must decide the number of students required to "get it" before instruction can proceed and which intervention to use for those who "didn't get it.") If anonymity is a concern, there is the option of having students close their eyes before they hold up their colors. Teachers can also have students leave the green side up in front of them on their desks and then discreetly turn over the note to the red to signal the teacher that they need more help. Using this strategy is a very quick way for the teacher to gather data to inform the next instructional steps.

For example, in Spanish class, Mrs. Mendez asks her students to keep their flippers (her word for the back-to-back red and green sticky notes) on their desks. As she introduces new vocabulary, students raise their red flipper if they have a question or to signal that they need repetition of the word.

For sorting. Another way teachers can use sticky notes to gather pre-assessment data is to ask students to write things they know about an upcoming topic on notes and then post these notes on a larger display board in ways that group or organize the information. Larger-size notes written on with markers are more effective for group viewing.

There are many variations teachers might try. Mrs. Berry uses sticky-note sorting to find out what students in 7th grade Family and Consumer Sciences know about fruits and vegetables before she begins her lesson on botanical categories. She gives students prepared sticky notes on which she's written the names of various fruits and vegetable. Students then must decide whether to post the note on a piece of chart paper labeled "Fruit" or on one labeled "Vegetable." The sorting generates some interesting conversation on whether tomatoes are fruits or vegetables and tells Mrs. Berry what information she should focus on in her lesson. After the lesson, she asks students to re-sort the fruit sticky notes into pones, drupes, seeds, melons, and citrus and the vegetable notes into roots, stems, flowers, leaves, seeds, and tubers. This visual display remains up throughout the unit to support discussion of differences in cooking techniques for tubers versus leaves, as well as instruction about nutritional values.

For analysis. On the taxonomy of learning, analysis is in the upper part of the pyramid. Sticky notes can be used prior to planned instruction to elicit evidence of students' analytical ability. For example, information can be broken down into parts, classified by attribute, prioritized, or compared and contrasted using multicolored slips. All approaches will serve to identify incoming gaps in knowledge.

To gain insight into the analytical thinking level of students in his American studies class, Mr. Rossi asks them to think about the best way for schools to go about educating students. He prompts them to think about how they learn and how schools can do the best job of teaching all children. Students write their responses on sticky notes.

Notice that Mr. Rossi chooses to approach this pre-assessment task via a subject he's sure all his students know well: school and the experience of being a student. After students have responded, he explains that cognitive systems focus on teaching to the head (i.e., knowledge, thinking, problem solving), behavioral systems focus on reward and punishment, and sociocultural systems factor in all the influences on learning and behavior that students bring to school from their larger world and that affect the culture of a school. When he's finished his explanation, he asks the students to sort their sticky-note responses into the category they believe is the best match by posting the notes on one of three pieces of poster board. This posting activity gives Mr. Rossi insight into students' higher-level analysis skills—that is, their ability to sort information by category.

In Mrs. Sanchez's class, students are working on a preliminary unit on multiple intelligences prior to selecting long-term research topics. Based on a series of questions, they identify their own strengths and skills on sticky notes and then sort them into each of Howard Gardner's multiple intelligences (MI). This can help students set the stage for a study of MI using very concrete examples. Once students identify their own types of intelligence, they use this information to design their projects in very personalized ways.

For engagement. Sticky notes can also be used to ensure that every student makes a contribution to the pre-assessment activity (or any activity, for that matter). A teacher could use them, for example, to elicit input from all students on their priorities for a particular unit of study. Mr. Wang expects the students in his business class to select a business career that they want to learn about. They write their ideas on sticky notes and post them on a brainstorming board. The ideas can be grouped by the type of job such as financial, creative, technology related, and so forth. Mr. Wang then uses this information to decide which careers to study as a whole class and which to assign to individuals. If a majority of the students want to learn more about artistic directors and marketers, but only a few want to learn about accountants and actuaries, Mr. Wang can respond accordingly.

Considering that they're nothing more than slips of paper with a little adhesive, sticky notes are a surprisingly powerful tool. Their key strength is their versatility and their ability to support many other formative assessment strategies in the lexicon. Teachers can use them as graphic organizers for color-coding objects or ideas that belong together, or they can use them for voting. I will discuss these uses and others in the next chapter on using formative assessment during instruction.

REFLECT AND APPLY

Here are some suggestions for using sticky notes in various content areas. How might the data generated contribute to the teacher's understanding of students' knowledge and skills? Their attitudes and beliefs? How might a teacher use the resulting data to inform instructional plans?

- *Reading:* Highlight text with color-coded strips. Label examples of symbolism or where the author shows point of view. Note page number and post/compare with others.
- *Science:* Ask students to sort bones into long and short by labeling on color-coded notes.
- *Interdisciplinary:* Post a main idea or concept and have students add color-coded notes. Add arrows and lines to show relationships.

Your turn: What are some ways you might use sticky notes to pre-assess students' knowledge, skills, or beliefs in your own classroom?

Responding Instructionally

Teachers have many options for responding to information from pre-assessments. But before responding, it's essential to organize and analyze the data collected so that you have the most accurate picture of what the class already knows, doesn't know, and needs to work on. These data will support decisions about how to adjust instruction to improve learning outcomes. In this section, I have listed several key questions to guide your work with pre-assessment data. Note that these questions can also be asked, with some adaptation, to guide the instructional decision making related to formative assessment during and after instruction (see Chapters 4 and 5).

Ask Yourself: What Information Do I Have? What Does It Mean?

The first set of questions focuses on data and data interpretation:

- What does the information from the pre-assessment mean? How do I interpret it?
- Does the information shed light on students' mastery of facts or skills?
- Does it provide insight into their beliefs or dispositions?
- What attitudes or levels of understanding, proficiency, or mastery do my students currently demonstrate?

Organizing pre-assessment data into a chart or table is a good way to gain an overview of students' knowledge or skill levels. For example, Ms. Dix, a 9th grade algebra teacher, knows her students must have an understanding of fractions, decimals, percents, and basic mathematical operations to be successful in her class. She pre-assesses her students to see where they are for each standard. The information will help her decide the starting point for instruction. Should she start with new concepts or first work on foundation competencies? Where will she set her baselines for competency? At a certain level of correct answers on a pre-test? And how many students must meet the set baseline target? Figure 3.1 is a table of Ms. Dix's pre-assessment data, showing what percentage of students she considers *proficient, partially proficient,* or *not proficient* in each standard.

FIGURE 3.1	Sample Pre-assessment Data		

Pre-assessment results for Ms. Dix's 9th grade algebra students
Entry Data: Standards Proficiency

Proficiency	% Not Proficient	% Partially Proficient	% Proficient
Standard 1: Basic operations	5	15	80
Standard 2: Fractions	12	28	60
Standard 3: Decimals	25	45	30
Standard 4: Percents	21	49	30

Ask Yourself: What Do the Students Need to Know and Do at This Point?

This second set of questions focuses on students' immediate needs, both as a group and as individuals:

- What level of understanding, proficiency, or mastery must each student have in order to move forward with the planned instruction?
- How many (and which) students have the requisite skills and entry knowledge to proceed with instruction?

After determining the percentages of students at each proficiency level, Ms. Dix, our algebra teacher, can see which standards need more attention. She can consider what target mastery percentages she would like to reach for each standard and which of her students she thinks have enough learning to move forward. The trigger points for how many need to achieve and at what level will vary by teacher, content area, and district. In some cases, a higher level of achievement in core knowledge and skills is required in order to move forward with instruction. For example, if a pre-assessment shows that not every student is able to demonstrate adequate knowledge about laboratory safety, then labs will not be part of instruction until they all reach proficiency. Each teacher's instructional design should map out the levels of achievement students are expected to reach and the associated instructional response when students do or do not measure up to these benchmarks.

Ask Yourself: How Do I Use the Data?

The third set of questions focuses on action, decisions, and adjustments:

• How can I decide which data are most educationally significant and defensible?
  • What steps can I take to respond to the pre-assessment data?
  • How do I adjust my teaching so that all students can be successful?

Ms. Dix uses the pre-assessment data to guide instructional content and rate of delivery as well as to plan selected interventions for her class. Based on her analysis, she decides to do a whole-class review of decimals and percentages, embed more fractions in the curriculum, and give students with less proficiency in basic operations some specialized instruction by grouping them together for a mini-lesson on foundations. As instruction proceeds, she continues using assessment in a formative manner to guide decisions and measure student progress against her pre-assessment data.

It's important that a teacher be open-minded yet opportunistic when looking at the documentation of students' incoming abilities. Flexibility is key in making adjustments to instruction. Remember, because you are using ongoing formative assessment, you will continue to receive more information about how effective your responses are in improving learning and can fine-tune them further by

• Changing a particular lesson plan in the unit
• Selecting different or additional resources
• Using different instructional strategies

- Identifying specific students in need of remediation
- Customizing rubrics to personalize the weight of the mastery of selected standards
- Grouping students homogeneously for differentiation or in heterogeneous groups for collaborative learning
- Changing the planned summative assessments

REFLECT AND APPLY

We will discuss gathering, using, and acting on data in more depth in Chapter 7. For now, choose a pre-assessment strategy and think about a unit of study in your curriculum. What data could you glean from using this pre-assessment strategy? What would your target learning goals be, and what instructional responses might you make?

■ ■ ■

Case Studies for Analysis

As you read the following case studies, reflect on what you have learned so far to determine whether the teacher's practices represent defensible formative assessment. What is the teacher doing to pre-assess? Are the pre-assessments nonthreatening, engaging, and revealing about prior knowledge, skills, or beliefs? Does the teacher use the data to adjust or differentiate instruction? How many different strategies can you identify?

Consider each of these main points in your analysis and evaluate the case study. Compare your ideas to the analysis given at the end of each study.

Case Study 1

Mrs. Chavez began her English class by asking a series of questions about a short novel that students were reading: "How does the theme of this book compare to that of previous books we've read?" "Which character is most important to the storyline?" "In what ways are the settings in this novel similar to those of others that we've read?" Her purpose was to identify baseline understanding of themes and characters.

Students recorded their responses on a grid that provided a box for each question and then found a classmate to share ideas with and complete their individual response sheets. During this dyad sharing time, Mrs. Chavez walked around and listened for students' understanding and gaps in knowledge. She asked some probing questions, such as "How would you describe this character's personality?" and "Why do you think the author chose this place and time?"

After a few minutes, she asked all students to take their sheets to an assigned group of three to share and compare responses. During this walk-about, Mrs. Chavez paid particular attention to selected students who had demonstrated gaps in understanding during the first pairing. In the triads, students shared the work from their dyads and then developed one collaborative response to each question. Each group posted its answers on sheets of newsprint tacked to the bulletin board and labeled: "Character," "Theme," and "Setting." After all the students had time to read the other triads' responses, the teacher asked them to look for areas of commonality and to use a SMART Board to compile the responses and develop one collaboratively agreed-upon response to each question. Students made corrections to their individual sheets, and at the end of the lesson, students completed an exit slip explaining what they had learned, relearned, or been reminded of regarding the key literary concepts. Mrs. Chavez collected their individual work for review, planning to identify misunderstandings and determine interventions.

Ask yourself: Did Mrs. Chavez use a formative assessment? If so, what elements made it formative? Would you advise Mrs. Chavez to make any changes in her practice?

Analysis: This scenario has parts of formative assessment in it. Mrs. Chavez connected an initiation activity and lesson preview to students' prior learning, but it's not clear what she did with the information she gathered. During the activity, she circulated and listened attentively and then divided the students into mixed-ability triads. Students had choice when the stakes were low; when the learning became more consequential, they were put in thoughtfully assigned groups. Mrs. Chavez used collaboration to supplement and reinforce knowledge. At the end of instruction, students presented evidence of whole-class learning, but it wasn't clear which students needed additional review. To complete this lesson in a formative way, Mrs. Chavez would need to collect and analyze individual data, give feedback, and select responsive interventions.

Case Study 2

At the beginning of a statistics class, Mr. Smith asked students to go up to the board and post their answer to a selected homework question. After a quick review of the responses, Mr. Smith pointed out the three problems that had been answered correctly. He then asked one of the students who got it right to share her process with the others. The other students self-corrected their work. Mr. Smith pointed out any particularly troublesome places in the problem, asked if there were any other questions, and then began the next lesson.

Ask yourself: Did Mr. Smith use a formative pre-assessment? What would you recommend that Mr. Smith do differently to get the most out of assessment in his classroom?

Analysis: Although Mr. Smith could determine which students understood the problem and which did not, he didn't offer any interventions. If it was clear that the majority of the class missed an idea, then there needed to be an instructional adjustment. When the data indicate certain students "don't get it," it is important to determine whether each student's incorrect response truly reflects a lack of understanding or is a computational error. None of this was obvious in the scenario. While Mr. Smith did gather data, he made minimal use of it.

CHAPTER 4

Formative Assessment During Instruction

You may have heard the traditional Buddhist fable about the blind men and the elephant. Each man touched a different part of the animal and declared what he thought he was feeling: a snake (the elephant's tail), a fan (the elephant's ear), a tree trunk (the elephant's leg), and a pipe (the elephant's tusk). Each of these men declared his perception to be the truth. The lesson behind this story is that each of us is apt to see the world from our own perspective. Although all teachers endeavor to present students with "the whole elephant" when they deliver instruction, they do not necessarily know how students perceive that elephant or what conclusions students are drawing.

Ongoing Assessment for Ongoing Learning

Learning is not a simple forward-moving process, which is why ongoing monitoring is essential. Your students come to you with various levels of prior knowledge and skills and with different values and beliefs; all these factors influence how they "see the elephant"—that is, how they will respond to instruction and the pace and pathways their learning will take. Over the course of a class, students often experience some backpedaling and wheel spinning as well as forward movement.

Although you may have adjusted your teaching plan in response to preassessment results, inevitable variations in student learning mean that you will need to keep measuring learning and adjusting your teaching throughout instruction. In a Web seminar on formative assessment, Rick Wormeli (2006a) referred to the continuous checking of student comprehension as formative "dipsticking." I prefer to think of it as temperature-taking with a rapid-read thermometer. Both comparisons convey the idea that you won't be able to accurately judge the state of students' understanding unless you use an instrument to regularly measure it. Using instruments makes it easy to see the range of responses and observe the learning and understanding as they both increase and decrease.

This is a lesson some of us learn the hard way. Consider the example of Ms. Gough. In the last chapter, we saw her pre-assess her psychology students' knowledge and beliefs before beginning a unit on positive discipline strategies. She decided that instruction to follow would concentrate on two primary discipline concepts: (1) providing children with examples of good behavior and (2) parents guiding appropriate behavior.

At the beginning of the unit, Ms. Gough distributes a work-along sheet that describes goals, lists key vocabulary, explains assignments, and describes learning activities. However, her plans do not include checking for understanding during the instructional process. The unit features just one assessment: a summative test at the end, consisting of multiple-choice questions and case study analyses.

When Ms. Gough grades these tests, the results surprise her. Although the students did well on the selected-response part of the test, indicating they'd acquired an understanding of the research and theories, many responded to the case study scenarios by recommending the use of reprimands and time-outs—responses that indicate the students do not understand how to apply the research to practice. Ms. Gough is discouraged by the apparent gap between her instruction and students' understanding.

She reviews the test with students, but the unit is over, and there is new material to get to. She does not have time to reteach.

Benefits and Rationale

Assessing during instruction allows you to customize your teaching to match the current status of learning in the classroom. The information you gather helps you decide whether to backtrack to address points of confusion or to fast-forward to encourage higher-level thinking about a topic. It helps you decide whether to make these adjustments for the whole class, for subsets of the class, or for specific individuals.

Let's take a closer look at some of the benefits of assessing formatively during instruction.

"Quick Pulse" Measurements of Group Understanding

At any time during a lesson, a teacher can stop for a moment and use a focus question to get a quick measure of emerging learning. Students might signal their degree of understanding in multiple ways, from raising their hands to pressing an electronic clicker.

For example, in a botany class focused on building vocabulary on leaf structures, a teacher might pause during a PowerPoint presentation and ask for a show of hands on whether the outer layer of a leaf is called the epidermis or the cuticle. This strategy can show who is getting the main idea and who is not, and it can prompt the teacher to decide on effective remediation.

Insight into Individual Progress

Formative assessment helps teachers identify individual students who are struggling with particular concepts or applications and respond with personalized feedback, assistance, and redirection to get learning back on track.

For example, Ms. Bonnie asks students in her digital imaging lab to use three tools—blur, sharpen, and smudge—to design a solar system that includes three stars and two planets. They must also incorporate the previously learned design elements of color, balance, and movement. During a walkabout, Ms. Bonnie notes that although Marguerite's page has beautiful colors, the planets are sharp and edgy. In other words, Marguerite is not applying enough pressure with the smudging tool. It takes only a moment for Ms. Bonnie to remind Marguerite of the importance of using gentle pressure to blend out the rough edges while not making an image too blurry. As Ms. Bonnie continues to circulate around the room, she notices that Jorge's picture has all the planets in one corner; she stops to review the design element of balance with him. On her next cycle through the room, she notes improvement in both students' work.

Support for Benchmarking

Formative assessment supports benchmarking, the process of comparing learning outcomes goals to selected standards for the purpose of overall improvement. Insight into whole-class and individual progress gained through continually measuring understanding helps both the teacher and students identify strengths, points of confusion, and the additional skill and knowledge development that will further progress toward mastery.

Consider this 6th grade science objective: *Students will be able to classify insects into subcategories (e.g., butterflies, caterpillars, grasshoppers, beetles, bees, and ants) and distinguish them from non-insects, such as spiders and centipedes.* A teacher could use several types of formative assessment throughout instruction, each focused on determining if and how well students are learning what they need to know to continue making progress. Can they identify an insect's various body parts? Do they know the physical characteristics of each of the subcategories of insect? Can they analyze these body parts' function in nature? In response to the data gathered through these assessments, the teacher can adjust instruction to ensure students acquire the skills and knowledge they need to master the standard.

Development of Critical Thinking Skills

Assessing during instruction can help teachers monitor how deeply students are understanding and thinking about a topic. Knowing at what level a student is processing new knowledge helps teachers choose appropriate instruction for the class and individuals.

The 6th grade science objective just mentioned—classifying insects—is part of a larger goal of many science curricula: recognizing that all of nature can be classified. Throughout the curriculum, comparisons are made among biological classifications, such as phylum, class, and genus. Formative assessment can provide insights into students' knowledge of these scientific classifications as well as their ability to analyze, synthesize, and apply learning.

Insight into Changes in Beliefs and Dispositions

If a teacher has pre-assessed to get a sense of students' dispositions or beliefs on a topic, assessing during instruction can reveal the degree to which students have changed their minds based on new information, research, or group discussion. Changes show teachers that students are absorbing and analyzing new content. For example, students in a financial literacy class may begin a unit thinking that people should not be allowed to declare bankruptcy under any circumstances and then modify that belief based on new understanding. If beliefs remain static, teachers may deduce that learning is stalled and take action to get it moving forward again.

Support for Student Self-Assessment

The ability to evaluate one's own performance or learning is a skill that develops slowly. Offering students opportunities to self-assess during a lesson furthers this competency. Student self-assessment also provides information about learning that is valuable to customizing instruction. Through formative assessment, teachers can bring to students' attention both areas that need more review and areas in which they are showing growth. Together, teachers and students can build a learning plan, which means setting goals and marking steps to reach those goals. Formative feedback during a unit also tells students that teachers are interested in them and their progress. In addition, including students in the assessment process tends to inspire a feeling of agency in their own learning.

REMEMBER

Use formative assessment during instruction to

- Take the pulse of whole-class progress
- Pinpoint individual achievement
- Benchmark learning
- Measure critical thinking
- Monitor changes in beliefs or dispositions
- Provide feedback and support self-assessment

Tools and Strategies for Assessing During Instruction

Formative assessment strategies are versatile and can be deployed to gather all kinds of information through a variety of response formats, including signaling, organizing and displaying, and questioning. Asking students to demonstrate their knowledge in different ways increases the chances that you will get an accurate picture of their understanding. Some students may be most comfortable explaining what they know in writing; others may be able to do this better through verbal explanations, by making graphic representations, or by signaling. Each of these formats has advantages for teachers too. Writing allows students to develop ideas and gives teachers a record of their thinking. Verbal responses give teachers an opportunity to follow up answers with more probing questions. Graphic displays make missing knowledge or lack of understanding about relationships readily apparent. And signaling can be silent and minimally disruptive to instruction.

As with pre-assessment strategies, the strategies I present in this chapter are flexible; they all can be adapted for different points in the instructional process and for different content areas. The seven tools and strategies I will discuss are Voting Cards, Fingers-Up, Line-Up, graphic organizers, Bump in the Road, questioning and the Socratic method, and electronic response systems, but you can find more strategies in the lexicon in Appendix B.

When selecting a strategy, keep in mind both the information you want to gather and how you could use it. Depending on the results your assessments generate, you might respond by personalizing instruction, differentiating lessons, or changing teaching strategies, or you might opt to develop corrective tutoring, create cooperative teams, or customize resources. We will turn to planning and instructional responses later in the chapter.

Voting Cards

Voting Cards—and other similar signaling-based strategies, such as Fingers-Up—is a no-fuss way to monitor learning and a good choice for fact checking, belief checking, or self-assessment. The teacher generally asks a yes/no, agree/disagree, or true/false question, and students use color-coded voting cards to show their responses: green for "yes," "agree," and "true"; red for "no," "disagree," and "false"; and yellow for "not sure." Students can make cards out of colored paper, or they can use sticky notes, painted Popsicle sticks, or wipe-off boards. The teacher might also distribute prepared answer cards with words keyed to the lesson content: *noun, verb,* and *adjective,* for example, or *imperméable, maillot,* and *pyjama.*

Along with other signaling strategies, assessment activities that use voting cards can be advantageous for shyer students, in that they allow them to participate without calling attention to themselves or having to hold the floor to respond. More boisterous signaling variations, such as having students cast their votes by clapping or stomping, can be a good choice when a lesson needs a burst of energy.

In practice: Mr. Blackburn uses the Voting Cards strategy to survey his students' stance on a variety of issues related to topics in his social studies class. For example, at several predetermined points during a lesson on immigrant rights, he asks students to vote on whether they agree (green card) or disagree (red card) that driver's licenses should be issued to undocumented immigrants. He surveys their pre-existing beliefs at the start of the lesson, groups students with common beliefs, and gives them an opportunity to share their views, research the facts on the topic, and come up with a collaborative justification for their position. Then, at the end of the collaborative work session, he takes a second "pulse," again asking students to signal their stance on the issue. Groups present their justification to the rest of the class. After all presentations are complete,

Mr. Blackburn asks students to once again signal their agreement or disagreement with issuing driver's licenses to undocumented immigrants so that he can see if any students have changed their position as a result of the new information.

As it happens, Mr. Blackburn does not see significant changes in students' stances on the issue at *any* of the voting stages. Frankly, it is a disappointing finding. Although the students had the opportunity to hone their research and synthesis skills (fulfilling one of his lesson objectives), another objective had been for students to expose themselves to new information and entertain a multiplicity of viewpoints before drawing a conclusion. Mr. Blackburn decides that his instruction would have been more effective if he had used the initial agree/disagree data from students' voting to form mixed-belief groups rather than common-belief groups. Requiring heterogeneous groups to reach consensus, he realizes, will expose students to a more diverse range of sources and points of view. He'll try that grouping arrangement next time.

REFLECT AND APPLY

Here are some sample voting questions for a range of content areas. How might the responses they generate contribute to the teacher's understanding of the status of class learning, individual achievement, and progress toward benchmarks? What kinds of responses might help to clarify the teacher's insight into students' critical thinking or self-assessment abilities? Imagine some of the vote counts the teacher might see. How might the teacher use the resulting data to adjust instruction? What follow-up questions might the teacher ask? What might the teacher's next steps be?

- *Science:* Will the wider of the two rubber bands stretched across the shoebox make the higher pitched sound? Hold up a green card to vote "yes," a red card to vote "no," and a yellow card to indicate "not sure."
- *Geometry:* Place a blue sticky note under the clock face that shows a supplementary angle and a yellow one under the clock face that shows a complementary angle.

- *Social Studies:* Who was it who said, "I regret that I have but one life to give for my country"? Was it Benedict Arnold, Patrick Henry, or Nathan Hale? Cast your vote by writing the person's name on your whiteboard.
- *French:* Which article of clothing would you wear to the beach? From your selection of cards, hold up the one with the name of the article written on it.

Your turn: Think of a lesson that you teach. How might you use voting cards to assess learning during instruction? What information could you seek, and what might you do with that information?

■ ■ ■

Fingers-Up

In Fingers-Up, teachers pose a question, and students use their fingers to signal their answer. They might hold up fingers: one to show agreement; two to show disagreement. They might hold up the number of fingers corresponding to their level of understanding on a scale of zero to five or to the number of examples or concept applications that they can think of.

This kind of body signaling has the advantage of adding movement to assessment, which stimulates the brain. As researcher Eric Jensen (2000) explains, "Movement does several things for the brain. It enhances circulation so that neurons get more oxygen and nutrients. It spurs the production of hormones that enhance brain function and it stimulates the production of dopamine, a mood enhancing neurotransmitter" (p. 167). So asking your students to stand up, sit down, raise hands, hold up fingers, and shake, wave, or pump fists helps their thinking, which, in turn, gives you the most accurate picture of their learning.

In practice: Mrs. Kim uses Fingers-Up several times during her 6th grade math lesson on applying fractions. After an initiation that includes a review of the basics of fractions, she asks students to hold up fingers to indicate how many ways they can think of to use fractions in daily life. She encourages every student to think of at least one application and waits until all students have raised at least one finger. Then she calls on individuals to share a use they have thought of. If other students have thought of the same application, they put one finger down so examples won't be repeated.

Mrs. Kim calls first on students who are holding up fewer fingers to make sure they will have a chance to contribute. In a notebook, she writes down the uses as students share them, noticing that there are more correct applications than incorrect ones and making note of the few students whose responses indicate they might need help. Then, she moves forward with the lesson, which includes a brief review of using fractions in cooking and gardening.

Later in the lesson, Mrs. Kim returns to the student-generated responses in her notebook and uses the data to create mixed-readiness groups. She tasks the groups with finding examples of fractions in the classroom and the school building. During the presentations that follow, students vote on the appropriateness of the examples the groups present by holding up one finger if they agree that it uses fractions or two fingers if they disagree that it uses fractions.

This assessment gives Mrs. Kim two types of information: (1) whether the students understand fractions well enough to find examples of them and (2) whether they can accurately evaluate one another's examples of fractions. Mrs. Kim is then able to double back to address points of misunderstanding, proceed to additional instruction on fractions (such as multiplying and dividing them), or move on to focus on percents and decimals.

The validity of this type of self-reporting assessment depends on the honesty of the students' responses. The more comfortable students feel in a classroom environment, the more likely they are to be honest—and unembarrassed—about what they do and do not understand. This feeling of safety tends to develop over time, as students become more familiar with formative assessment procedures. On a practical level, teachers can promote privacy and encourage reluctant signalers through simple means such as asking students to close their eyes when they signal.

Sometimes students are reluctant to participate in signaling not because of potential embarrassment but because of a cultural predisposition. For example, Mrs. Jacobi noticed that several students in her class rarely held up their hands and fingers when she asked them to signal. Her school was in a community with a large immigrant population, and as Mrs. Jacobi learned more about her reluctant signalers and their culture, she discovered that they were hesitant to share their own knowledge with others because their culture discouraged self-promotion and placed a low value on personal recognition. After she asked the students to make flags of their families' countries of origin and hold up these instead of a hand or a finger, Mrs. Jacobi noticed a marked increase in signaling. Her students were readily willing to show their pride in their group's nationality as a way to indicate their own learning.

REFLECT AND APPLY

Here are some sample questions for Fingers-Up in a range of content areas. How might the responses they generate contribute to the teacher's understanding of the status of class learning, individual achievement, and progress toward benchmarks? Would they reveal critical thinking or support self-assessment?

- *Geometry:* Hold up your fingers to indicate how many sides there are in a parallelogram.
- *Literature:* Did Shakespeare write all his own plays? Hold up one finger for yes, five fingers for no.
- *Music:* How many wind instruments can you think of?

Your turn: Think of a lesson that you teach. How might you use Fingers-Up to assess learning during instruction? What are some possible ways to adjust your instruction in response to data gathered?

Line-Up

Line-Up provides a way to assess students' sequencing ability. *Sequencing* is identified in the synthesis section of Bloom's taxonomy as a way to organize knowledge. It can be used for putting things in order or arranging knowledge in a progression. It can also demonstrate how one thing has to come before another. One basic way to use it is to form groups and give each student in the group a prepared card on which you have printed an item or idea to put in chronological or sequential order. Students then arrange themselves in the order in which they think the information should be sequenced. Line-Up also works with multiple teams. The groups can compare and discuss their sequencing.

In practice: In Child Development, Mrs. Chatelle forms groups and gives each group member an index card on which she's written one of the four stages of Piaget's intellectual development. At her signal and without speaking, students line up, putting the stages in order. They use their fingers to communicate to each other their place in the sequence. Then each group shares their sequence, and other groups have the opportunity to comment.

In this scenario, Mrs. Chatelle gains insight into two levels of students' learning: (1) their ability to recall information and (2) their ability to evaluate each group's responses. She notices that although most of the sequences are accurate, some groups are unable to explain why these sequences had meaning for the study of children. She invites the groups that "got it" to quickly share their sequence again and asks a series of follow-up questions to ensure their reasoning is clear to all. She then moves the students to the next objective: applying Piaget's stages to the design of developmentally appropriate activities for young children.

REFLECT AND APPLY

Here are some sample sequencing problems in a range of content areas. How might the responses they generate contribute to the teacher's understanding of the status of class learning, individual learning, and progress toward benchmarks? Would they help to reveal critical thinking or self-assessment abilities?

- *Chemistry:* Place the elements in group one of the periodic table in the proper sequence.
- *History:* Arrange this sequence of events of the U.S. Civil War.
- *Culinary Arts:* Now that you all have your role assignments for our end-of-the-year dinner, line up in the order that reflects where your role fits into the overall sequence of planning, preparing, and serving the meal. Be prepared to explain your position in relation to the final outcome.

- *Technology:* Demonstrate the primary sequence for the creation of a PowerPoint presentation.

Your turn: Think of a lesson that you teach. How might you use Line-Up to assess learning during instruction?

■ ■ ■

Graphic Organizers

Graphic organizers, which include diagrams, mind maps, concept maps, tables, charts, matrixes, and semantic organizers, provide a window into students' thinking. They are a good choice for teachers who are interested in how students are categorizing and connecting information and who need to see if there are gaps in students' understanding. Graphic organizers are also particularly useful for whole-class brainstorming at the beginning and end of instruction, and used in this way, they provide insight into learning progress. And because many graphic organizer formats ask for and can support a lot of detail, they help provide a snapshot of students' critical thinking. Feedback, questions, and teacher interventions based on results can all serve to keep learning on track or help take it to new heights.

Teachers should determine the best organizer for their students and their specific subject area. Each format is somewhat flexible, and each, in its own way, can illuminate a student's thinking. Many Web sites offer templates of graphic organizers, and spending some time sorting through these is worthwhile. Here, I am going to describe three visual organizers—webs, Venn diagrams, and matrixes—and give examples of how to use them formatively.

Keep in mind that graphic organizers may serve a variety of instructive purposes but they aren't part of formative assessment unless you take the time to glean data from them and then put the data to use.

In practice: Teachers often ask students to use a web diagram to illustrate influencing factors or forces acting on something. Figure 4.1 shows a sample web from Mr. Wilson's history class, which students create as he delivers a lecture on the causes of war.

As Mr. Wilson speaks, he walks up and down the classroom rows, checking in to see the kind of information students are recording and getting a general sense of which students are following him well and which are not. After his lecture, he uses the informal assessment data to put students into heterogeneous groups for a Think–Pair–Share activity in which they reflect on, discuss, and expand their webs. Although they work as partners, each student is responsible for his or her own web. Meanwhile, Mr. Wilson circulates throughout the room, listening to the students' conversations and noting areas of understanding and confusion. For example, although he can hear and see that all student groups have identified economic factors as a cause for war, few groups have picked up on sociological causes. Knowing this understanding is critical, Mr. Wilson launches into a mini-lecture focused specifically on this topic before returning to the next activity in his prepared lesson plan: asking the pairs to expand their webs to include additional elements, such as tribal factors, control of banks, community norms, and elections.

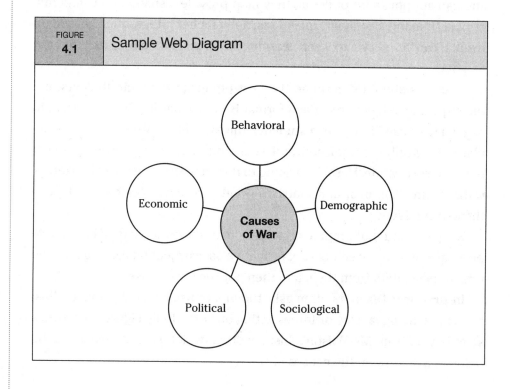

FIGURE 4.1	Sample Web Diagram

Teachers most frequently use Venn diagrams for compare-and-contrast exercises. During a lesson on cell structure, for example, Mrs. Jones asks students to compare and contrast the cell structure of plants and animals by filling out the Venn diagram in Figure 4.2. She collects this work, reviews each student's diagram, and provides individual feedback. She also uses this assessment to inform her grouping assignments for a WebQuest in which students must search for discrete pieces of information related to the topic they know the least about: cell walls, vacuoles, chloroplasts, ribosomes, or the Golgi apparatus.

Matrixes offer a way to gather data on student understanding at various stages in a lesson, revealing growth in learning to both teachers and students. For example, Mrs. Ruby gives the matrix in Figure 4.3 to her students at the beginning of her lesson on nutrition and asks them to fill out column 1 with what they already knew about nutrients. They go on to share their background knowledge in a round-robin format, and Mrs. Ruby listens for gaps in knowledge, stepping in occasionally to reinforce accurate information, provide additional details, and clarify misunderstandings. Of course, some students claim they already know everything about nutrition. Mrs. Ruby uses probing questions to lead students who have a good degree of nutrition knowledge to a deeper understanding. Students take notes during this discussion, adding information to column 2 and

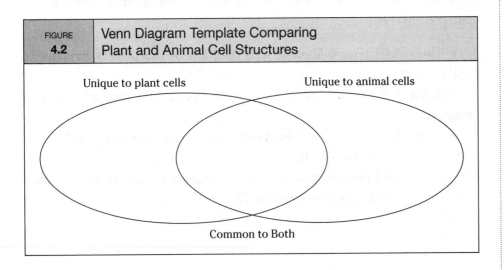

| FIGURE 4.2 | Venn Diagram Template Comparing Plant and Animal Cell Structures |

Unique to plant cells

Unique to animal cells

Common to Both

FIGURE 4.3	Matrix of Incoming Knowledge and Learning Application		
Nutrition Knowledge			
	Column 1 What I already know	**Column 2** What I learned in class	**Column 3** How I can use this learning to make healthy choices
Carbohydrates			
Protein			
Fats			
Vitamins			
Minerals			

assembling a strong foundation. They go on to fill in column 3 in collaborative groups.

In this example, a matrix serves multiple purposes, helping students organize information, display their knowledge, and record their new learning. It also provides them with an opportunity to apply their learning.

REFLECT AND APPLY

Teachers in all content areas can assess using graphic organizers. As you look over the sample assessments across content areas, try to picture what the displays might look like and what information teachers would gather from them.

- *Financial Literacy:* Make a web diagram of the factors influencing credit rating.
- *Science:* Sort characteristics of mollusks and fin fish using a Venn diagram.
- *Social Studies:* In a Venn diagram, compare the causes of World War I to the causes of World War II.
- *Literature:* Using the provided cards, sequence the events of the lives of the main characters in *Love in the Time of Cholera.*

Your turn: How might you incorporate graphic organizers and other forms of visual display in a lesson? What information would you gather about learning? How could you use the display to support feedback to students?

■ ■ ■

Bump in the Road

In this strategy, teachers ask students to write down a point they find confusing about the topic of instruction: a "bump in the road" in their learning. The students must self-assess their own understanding and decide the cause of any confusion. Like a real speed bump, this strategy can slow down instruction long enough for students to think about what they have learned and to identify gaps in understanding. It provides an opportunity for reflection and feedback. Teachers can collect responses and use them to plan instruction, review them individually with students and discuss possible ways to clear up foggy points, or place students in groups and ask them to share and discuss their "bumps." If everyone in a group is confused by the same point, the group shares the bump with the whole class. Note that the Bump in the Road strategy is essentially a self check-in. It is intended to illuminate areas of confusion or missing information. Other strategies that serve the same purpose are Feathers and Salt and Muddiest Point. A Quickwrite or Quickdraw can serve this purpose as well.

In practice: In Ms. Huertas's accounting class, she plans to follow her introduction of 10 key terms by asking students to comment on points of confusion. Are they, perhaps, struggling with the concepts of debits and credits? Do they grasp the differences between journals, ledgers, and balance sheets? If many students express confusion, she will review and reteach certain terms, varying her instruction to incorporate a different modality. If only a few students are uncertain, she plans to set aside time to work with them in small groups while the rest of the class proceeds to an applied ledger activity.

Here are some sample Bump in the Road questions for a range of content areas. How might the responses they generate contribute to the teacher's understanding of the status of class learning, individual achievement, and progress toward benchmarks? Would data reveal critical thinking or self-assessment abilities?

- *Health:* What don't you understand about the opposing viewpoints on teaching sex education in schools?
- *Biology:* Which aspect of the relationship of the anterior leg muscle to leg joints is the least clear to you?
- *Psychology:* Write or draw the part of axons, dendrites, and neurotransmitters that is most confusing to you.

Your turn: Think of a lesson that you teach. How might you use Bump in the Road or a similar student self-check strategy to assess learning during instruction?

Questioning and the Socratic Method

All of assessment relates to questioning. In asking students to identify, explain, or demonstrate what they know, the teacher can identify gaps, misinformation, and misuse of knowledge. As questions make the gaps readily apparent, teachers can devise strategies to fill in the missing information or correct procedural errors before these take on neurological permanence.

The Socratic method is a specific form of questioning set up as a dialogue of question and response. The teacher poses a question in order to probe student understanding. The student responds, and the teacher follows up with a question that prompts further exploration. Well-designed questions are also teaching tools, guiding students in thought and challenging them to use higher-order thinking skills. In using the Socratic method during instruction, teachers have both a measure of the learning taking place and a method to improve it.

Research has repeatedly documented the effectiveness of questioning, and studies show that teachers use it second only to lecturing as a teaching and assessing method. However, research also shows that the quality of questioning and the cognitive level of questions that most teachers use are typically at a lower than optimal level. Teachers are not getting all the information they can about student learning and achievement, and students are not being challenged to use higher-order thinking (Cotton, 2002).

Characteristics of skillful questioning. The kind of questioning that is most effective

- Engages students in learning
- Elicits display of students' thinking
- Nurtures new insights
- Encourages application of knowledge
- Promotes making connections, past/future and interdisciplinary
- Assesses learning
- Guides learning
- Encourages higher-order thinking

To reap these benefits, teachers must carefully design the questions they pose to students. First, they must decide the type of information they want to get from the question and then frame the question to yield that information. In order to assess students' higher-order thinking skills, teachers must use questions that correspond in level. I've listed some example questions here for each level of cognition in Bloom's taxonomy to illustrate how questioning can be used throughout a full cognitive range. As you read the questions, fill in the blanks with content from one of your own classes.

- *Knowledge:* Tell me three things you know about _____? What do you think _____ means? Give an example of _____. Label the following: _____.
- *Comprehension:* How does this relate to _____? What's important about _____? Tell me more about _____. Explain _____ in your own words.

- *Application:* In what situation can you use _____? Whom does _____ most affect? Predict the next step in or outcome of _____.
- *Analysis:* What would happen if _____? What is the evidence for _____? How do the parts of _____ compare/contrast to each other or to the whole?
- *Synthesis:* How can you _____? Put two of the ideas together for _____. Create a plan to _____. Propose a solution to this problem: _____.

Questioning is particularly effective in revealing the student's present ability to apply, analyze, and synthesize. But there is a trick to having students accurately demonstrate these abilities: wait time. Determining appropriate wait time is one of the hardest skills for new teachers to master, but providing it is one of the most effective ways to promote thinking and engagement. A three-second wait time is recommended, yet most teachers allow only one second. Waiting longer will elicit a greater range and depth of responses, thereby contributing to the effectiveness of questioning as a formative assessment tool.

Follow-up questions. Strong follow-up questions in response to students' answers can help reveal students' critical-thinking skills and further those skills' development. Here are some suggestions for questions that will help to probe understanding further:

- Can you express that idea another way?
- How can we check the accuracy of your statement?
- What is the relevance of that to _____?
- What other dimensions to this problem are there?
- What might be another point of view?
- Does your argument follow a logical sequence?

In practice: Students in Mr. Toshibi's social studies class have been studying the U.S. education system, weighing its pros and cons, and using this insight to design a better school. Midway through the project, Mr. Toshibi presents a small-group assignment: students working in "Reform

Groups" of eight will pair up into two-person subgroups to offer their ideas on the best way to redesign school technology use, school construction, teaching approaches, and school leadership. As the pairs brainstorm, Mr. Toshibi circulates around the room asking questions such as, "How do your ideas compare to the current education system?" and "What is the basis for these ideas?" He is careful not to ask students to defend their ideas; his purpose is to probe for their thinking.

After the brainstorming period, the subgroups report out and respond to their classmates' questions. "Remember," Mr. Toshibi says, "we're not judging the reform ideas here. We're asking questions for clarification and to promote everyone's understanding." After one subgroup advocates for schools without teachers, Mr. Toshibi asks them why. The pair responds that they could learn just as well on their own. The rest of the class has follow-up questions: "Without teachers, how would you know what you need to learn?" "How would you gain the needed knowledge and skills?" "How will you know when you've learned what you need to know?"

As these questions and others are posed and answered, Mr. Toshibi provides little direction beyond reminding students of the ground rules: "Again, we're prompting, not arguing." He does, however, ask a few follow-ups of his own, and he takes notes on the students' questions and responses, jotting down what these tell him about their thinking.

In an activity reliant on questioning, it is essential that teachers seek ways to delve deeper. Consider this example:

Teacher: At what point in the story did you begin to question Holden Caulfield's mental health?

Morgan: It's hard to know whether he's insane or just a confused teenager.

Meg: Oh, he's definitely crazy. Can't you see that?

Morgan: Then why is his sister the only person he doesn't think is phony?

Teacher: So are you saying that Holden is selective in his judgment of people? Why might this be? When you answer, consider the character traits of the people he judges.

Here's another:

Teacher: Recall what we said about antagonists and protagonists in a story. How does the author portray various characters in this book?

Thea: Holden is the protagonist, because he is the leading character.

Chou: No, he's the antagonist, because he is against everyone.

Teacher: Think about what you just said in relation to our definition of *protagonist* as the leading character in a literary work. You're right, it can be confusing, because antagonists can advocate against a social setting, as Holden does. But based on our class definition, can you see Holden's role?

Chou: Oh, yeah, I get it now.

Notice that this teacher's questioning responses to student questions assess level of understanding, probe for more information, reinforce accurate knowledge, and provide opportunities for adding to, changing, and adapting instruction. Formatively, teachers can use questioning to ensure learning has occurred at a lower level before moving on to target a higher level of thinking. Teachers can also group students to ask and respond to one another's questions. In responding, they not only demonstrate their new knowledge but also provide information for the teacher on their depth of learning and gaps in knowledge.

REFLECT AND APPLY

Here are some sample questions for using questioning and the Socratic method in a range of content areas. How might the responses they generate contribute to the teacher's understanding of the status of class learning, individual achievement, and progress toward benchmarks? Would data reveal critical thinking or self-assessment abilities? How might the teacher use this information to adjust instruction?

- *Government:* You've all talked about what you don't like about the current income, sales, and personal tax system. What do you think would be a better or fairer system of taxation?
- *Biology:* What influences our basal metabolism rate and which of those factors can you control? What questions do you have about the ones that can be controlled?

- *World History:* What is the relationship between religion and war? Can you give three examples in history to illustrate your points?

Your turn: Think of a lesson that you teach. How might you use questioning in general—and the Socratic method in particular—to assess learning during instruction? What are some possible ways to adjust your instruction in response to data gathered?

■ ■ ■

Electronic Response Systems

From the dynamic interaction of questioning, we turn to the quiet privacy of electronic response systems, such as the clickers and remotes that are now available. With these technologies, students can vote or respond privately during instruction, giving teachers ongoing feedback about learning. Teachers use electronic response systems much like they use Voting Cards, Fingers-Up, or other signaling strategies to poll the audience, ask questions, and collect data. The data, in turn, can be interpreted and used to modify instruction, reteach, and plan assessment. Responder sessions can be student paced or teacher paced, and they can be preplanned or done on the fly. Teachers can align these with standards and track responses over time. Reports can be customized for the teacher, grade, or school. Collectively, these new electronic technologies have the potential to be wonderfully effective formative assessment tools.

In practice: Mr. Biswas, who teaches music, uses electronic responders during a lesson on song structure. He asks students to listen to selected songs and click in when they hear the introduction, the first verse, the chorus/refrain, and the bridge. As the lesson continues, the music selections became more complex, and Mr. Biswas asks them to add other components of composition to their signaling. During a different lesson, he asks students to click to identify the next note in a chord and to identify key signatures.

Here are some sample questions for using electronic response systems in a range of content areas. How might the responses they generate contribute to the teacher's understanding of the status of class learning, individual achievement, and progress toward benchmarks? Would data reveal critical thinking or self-assessment abilities? How might the teacher use this information to adjust instruction?

- *Math:* Convert three-fourths to a percent.
- *Science:* Which one of the following is not an amino acid?
- *Social Studies:* The United States was right to have invaded Iraq: yes or no?
- *Spanish:* Identify the verb in this sentence.

Your turn: Think of a lesson that you teach. How might you use electronic responses to assess learning during instruction? What are some possible ways to adjust your instruction in response to data gathered?

Responding Instructionally

As noted, assessment data become formative assessment data when teachers use them to inform instructional decisions. Here are seven key questions that can help you decide on appropriate instructional responses:

1. What does your data mean? Does it provide insight into students' factual knowledge, skills mastery, or beliefs/disposition?

2. With respect to the instructional objective, what level of understanding or mastery do students currently demonstrate?

3. At this stage of instruction, what level of understanding or mastery must students have to continue progress toward attaining the instructional objective?

4. At this time, what percentage of (and which) students have attained the necessary level of understanding or mastery?

5. At this time, which and how many students are not ready to move on?

6. What are appropriate instructional responses to these findings? How will they address the needs of all students—both those who have attained mastery and those who have not?

7. How will the effectiveness of these responses be determined? What assessment strategies will be used, and when?

In my own research (Greenstein, 2005), I've found that when teachers are confronted with reluctant or struggling learners, their primary strategy is to reteach. However, they explain, their reteaching is often eerily similar to their first, less-than-successful round of teaching. When assessment results indicate a gap in learning, it is essential to change the instructional strategies. This section looks at a number of effective approaches to consider.

REMEMBER

Instructional responses to formative assessment data can include

- Changing a particular lesson plan in the unit
- Selecting different or additional resources
- Using different instructional strategies
- Identifying specific students in need of one-on-one remediation
- Customizing rubrics to personalize the weight of the mastery of selected standards
- Grouping students homogeneously for differentiation or in heterogeneous groups for collaborative learning
- Changing the planned summative assessments

Make the Content More Accessible

There are a number of ways to help students connect with content. If you believe readiness is a factor, your response might be to focus on smaller or simpler sets of skills and help students build toward the more challenging content. You might also take a look at the learning materials and resources you're using and ensure they're a good match for your students.

For example, Mr. Perkins concludes, based on data gathered through signaling and Muddiest Point, that variations in his earth science students' reading abilities are what's keeping some of them from understanding the main idea of biodiversity. A number of terms in the textbook—such as *ecosystem, biotic,* and *abiotic*—appear to be beyond their current comprehension levels, and Mr. Perkins suspects that the process of struggling with the textbook is turning them off and shutting down their learning. His response is to contact the textbook publisher and get preview copies of similar books written at an easier reading level. His purpose is to remove barriers and allow struggling students better access to the course content.

Adjust Pace or Sequence

If assessment data gathered during instruction indicate that all students understand the material, you might skip a planned explanation or activity and move directly to the next topic; if more are lost or struggling, you can slow down, providing additional practice or skills-based drills, perhaps, or allowing more time for questions and clarification.

Consider, too, the sequence of content and how you might alter it to boost students' interest and investment in the material or otherwise support their understanding. It's true that in some subject areas there are logical sequences that require strict adherence. Students need to learn about place value before they can take on decimals, for example, and some historical events definitely should be studied in chronological order. However, often the instructional sequence teachers follow is a holdover from curriculums of the past. Material is taught in a certain order because "that's how we've always done it." In these cases, students might very well benefit from a different approach. For example, if there is a contentious mayoral race under way in town, is there any reason why a social studies teacher shouldn't take advantage of it, skip ahead to a unit on local government, and then circle back to a unit on federal government? Is there any reason why a 7th grade life sciences teacher must teach plants before mammals?

Change the Setting

Changing the learning setting—from whole-class instruction to group work or from one kind of grouping arrangement to another—is another possible response to formative assessment data. Remember that groups can be homogeneous or heterogeneous, based on skill level or interest, and assigned or self-selected, depending on the lesson and desired learning outcomes. When using mixed groups for an applied or authentic assignment, students can work together to create a product, such as a poster, provided that each student is evaluated based on his or her individual contribution. When teachers want to work with students on specific knowledge or skills, homogeneous grouping makes sense.

Provide Specific Feedback and Opportunities for Choice

Giving students information about their progress is an important part of formative assessment. Muir (2001) found that students who believe their teachers are interested in their learning and in helping them succeed are more highly motivated. Motivation is a complex topic. It is closely tied to self-efficacy, which is defined as a belief about one's ability to be productive and effective. As Bandura (1994) puts it, "Self-efficacy beliefs determine how people feel, think, motivate themselves, and behave" (p. 72). Students with a high degree of self-efficacy are more likely to challenge themselves, believe that a lack of success is something they can personally remediate, and recover quickly from setbacks. Students with a lower degree of self-efficacy believe they cannot be successful and, therefore, avoid challenges. They also tend to blame their failures on external forces beyond their control.

Carol Dweck (2002) found that feedback, rather than praise, seemed to make the most difference in students' sense of self-efficacy. Praise merely stated that they were good at something; feedback indicated strengths, weaknesses, and strategies for improvement. On a practical level, then, providing feedback to struggling students doesn't just help them "get back on course" for the lesson or content at hand, it also helps lay the foundation for future success.

Another way to build students' feelings of competence is to give them choices about how to approach learning goals. With independent learning, such as projects or WebQuests, there are always standards to be met and rubrics to measure up to. Giving students a choice on the means they will take to achieve the required ends supports the ideas of multiple intelligences and differentiation in ways that build student confidence. Feedback, in these cases, will align with the targeted standards.

Individually, when a student is struggling with material, the teacher can sit with him or her and discuss strategies for approaching an assignment. Another approach is to ask the student what he or she might need to do differently in order to make progress. Together, the teacher and student might identify strategies such as completing homework, asking more questions, taking better notes, and checking in with the teacher after class to go over points of confusion.

Making students partners in measuring their progress, in coming up with responses to setbacks or gaps in learning, and in setting learning goals all improve self-efficacy (Margolis & McCabe, 2006), and all are an integral part of the formative classroom. This is something teachers must consider during the instructional planning process.

Planning for Learning

One key to successful formative assessment is embedding measures of learning into the instruction provided. To help ensure that you assess formatively and respond instructionally, I recommend including formative assessment activities and possible responses in your lesson plans. I also recommend sharing a summary of your unit plans with students. This "work-along," as I call it, is a way for them to prepare to learn and to participate in the monitoring of that learning.

Lesson Plans

Teachers tend to collect lesson plans. Some of these may be pet plans that we use frequently, while others may be used more sporadically, perhaps without any solid data for their effectiveness. When designing lesson plans with formative assessment in mind, teachers must embed measures not only of student learning but also of the effectiveness of instruction.

Figure 4.4 is a template for planning a lesson that incorporates frequent formative assessment. It includes the lesson components, examples of effective strategies, and the rationale for each component. Please bear in mind that not every lesson will include every element.

Let's look at some examples of how teachers might use the template.

Although pre-assessment and initiations are listed as separate components on the template, they can be combined in one activity. A pre-assessment can both generate data about prior knowledge and get student attention before instruction. Both functions prime the brain for learning. Consider this example, from Mr. Phillips's Modern History course. He begins a unit on the Vietnam War with an entrance-slip pre-assessment.

FIGURE 4.4	Formative Lesson Plan Template	

Unit:
Goal/Standard:
Objective:

Concept	Strategy	Rationale
Attention Grabber	Examples: Brainteaser, icon	Establishes a positive tone and anticipatory mind-set
Connections to Prior Learning	Review of prior lesson or earlier experience	Begins to establish meaning and form patterns
Pre-assessment	Examples: Entrance Slips, K-W-L, Voting Cards, Corners, Gallery	Identifies rudimentary knowledge and potential gaps
Initiation	Examples: Goals and objectives, new content, relevance of the topic, a story or case study, snippet of a video	Previews new learning, focuses the upcoming learning, and captures students' interest
Instruction	Teacher (or media) delivery of content and skills; consider challenge levels, pacing, and learning links	Provides opportunity to engage multiple intelligences, differentiate instruction
Embedded Formative Assessment	Examples: Graphic organizers, Quickdraw/Quickwrite, Nutshelling, Think–Pair–Share	Monitors learning during instruction
Application, Activity, Practice	Examples: Experiments, skits, games, write a story, create, produce	Provides practical application and stimulates the kinesthetic and social brain
Memory Prompts	Examples: Mnemonic, song, memory cards, visual images	Embeds learning
Reflection	Examples: Journal, self-evaluation, future needs assessment	Personalizes meaning
Post-assessment	Common formative assessment	Informs teaching and learning

The results show that 80 percent of his students don't know when the Vietnam War took place and the other 20 percent have a relative who fought in the war and know dates and events related to it.

To prime the class for the learning to come, Mr. Phillips shows a snippet of *The Deer Hunter,* which he follows with a whole-class review of basic facts. Then he differentiates his instruction, dividing the 80 percent of the class who have little prior knowledge of the war into groups to review news headlines from the period and tasking the remaining 20 percent with planning and setting up interviews with their family members who are veterans of the war. At the next class session, the groups share their headlines and interviews in an instructional round-robin format. After a brief discussion, each student writes something important he or she knows about the war on a sticky note and posts it on a "Vietnam Wall."

Thanks to this Gallery assessment, Mr. Phillips can see that, collectively, the members of his class have a large array of knowledge. What he doesn't see, however, are patterns in the information. Although they have lots of facts and feelings about the Vietnam War, they don't have an organized understanding of it. He responds by asking students to brainstorm ways they might group the information on the wall. Together, they come up with these categories: time line, geography, politics, and opposition to the war. Mr. Phillips goes on to use these four categories as the basis for the next applied activity: creating an issue of a Vietnam-era newspaper, with all students making contributions based on individual research.

Mr. Phillips sets up formative check-ins throughout the newspaper project. He reviews research notes and provides feedback, and he has students conduct peer reviews of each others' story rough drafts. Students keep an inverted pyramid of information as they work. By summative test time, both groups know core facts and have a deep understanding of the sociopolitical conditions of the day.

After the main facts and ideas of a lesson are presented through an instructional activity, such as a lecture or PowerPoint presentation, a teacher can ask students to sort and organize the information through a graphic organizer or another kind of assessment. In her American History class, for example, Mrs. Jarvis divides students into heterogeneous groups (a purposeful mix of high-achieving students and struggling learners) to create T charts comparing the key beliefs of the Jeffersonian Republicans and the Federalists. As the members of the group discuss the issues, each student makes an individual chart to be used for review. Mrs. Jarvis also reviews these charts, using them as formative assessment data and the basis for feedback. After noting collective gaps in learning, she cycles back to a teacher presentation and then uses a Muddiest Point activity.

In a formative assessment classroom, this kind of activity is typically followed by an assignment where students practice and apply their learning through individual or group activities. At this time, the teacher might take another quick-pulse measurement. In an anatomy class, for example, after a lecture on the digestive system, students might be given a poster of this system and asked to embark on a scavenger hunt to find and label the system's various organs. During the assessment workshops I teach, I place a paper bag on each table. In the bags are slips of paper; on some, I've written assessment terms, and on others, I've provided the definitions of those terms. After the teachers seated at each table have reviewed the definitions of assessment, measurement, balanced assessment, formative assessment, and summative assessment, they remove the slips from the bag and match each term to its definition. They compare their results to a correct posting and have the opportunity to ask clarifying questions of me and of the other teachers at their table. It's an exercise that points out where their gaps in knowledge lie and then gives them the opportunity, via discussion, to fill in those gaps.

REMEMBER

When planning a lesson, include

- A pre-assessment activity
- An initiation
- Instruction or method of delivering content and skills
- Assessments during instruction
- Application and practice activities
- Memory prompts
- A self-assessment or reflection activity
- A post-assessment

Work-Alongs

The students' counterpart to the lesson plan is the work-along. It is both a tool and a continuous and collaborative approach to monitoring and tracking learning that provides clear direction to students and supports personalization. At the start of a unit, each student gets a sheet that combines a pre-assessment (e.g., an entrance slip), a list of unit objectives, an initiation activity that requires a response on the sheet, empty outlines to be filled in during instruction, assignments, lists of assessments and attached directions and rubrics, and a post-instruction assessment (e.g., an exit slip). Figure 4.5, a sample work-along for a unit on child development, includes all of these components.

Students keep the work-along as the first sheet in their notebooks, and as the unit progresses, teachers can either collect the work-alongs for review or lead a discussion of students' progress (or wheel spinning) so far. Early in this process, it becomes evident where the gaps between the students' incoming knowledge and the achievement standards are. This evidence forms the foundation for deciding what to teach, how to teach, and where to differentiate both instruction and assessment.

Throughout the unit, as students continue to follow the work-along, the teacher continues to use it to decide when to slow down, speed up, or make other adjustments to instruction. For example, when Ms. Walsh notes that her students have a good grasp at the knowledge level, she adjusts the summative test to include more extended-response questions, such as essays, applied case studies, and analyses of reading.

There is some professional disagreement as to whether completion of the work-along should factor in a student's grade. Some advocate counting only the summative assessment at the end of the unit (Wormeli, 2006a), while others are more flexible in considering work along the way (O'Connor, 2007). I believe that work in progress should have some weight in grading. If the planning and tracking of the work-along are modeled, valued, and graded, then completing it becomes important to students. Teachers can also weight assessments, assignments, and activities individually for students right on their sheets or offer students choices of which ones to complete. These sheets keep students involved in monitoring their progress from start to finish and provide direction and clarity to their learning. They give teacher and students valuable informative feedback throughout the unit.

FIGURE 4.5	Sample Student Work-Along

Course: Teaching the Young Child
Unit: Physical Growth and Development

What do you know about babies' physical needs and development?

1. _____

2. _____

3. _____

What do you want to learn about the physical care and growth of babies?

1. _____

2. _____

3. _____

Unit Objectives

1. Describe the physical growth and abilities of children from newborns to 3-year-olds.

2. Demonstrate ways to meet the physical care (feeding, bathing, dressing, sleep, safety) and needs of infants.

3. Differentiate between small and large motor skills.

4. Select toys and activities that meet the physical growth needs of infants and toddlers.

Activities

Initiation

1. What are three needs (not wants) that children have when they are born? These can be physical, social, emotional, or intellectual. Compare your ideas to those in the text (Chapter 7, pp. 237–239). Discuss with your group why each person's ideas are similar or different.

_____

_____

_____

2. Describe a newborn's appearance. (Use Chapter 7.3, pp. 236–237, for reference.)

_____

_____

_____

(Continued)

FIGURE 4.5	Sample Student Work-Along *(Continued)*

Objective 1

3. Watch the PowerPoint presentation and define the following reflexes:

Rooting _____

Grasp _____

Startle _____

Moro _____

Objective 2

4. Infant Care Demonstrations: The assignment and rubric are provided on a separate sheet. (Use Chapters 6.2, 8.3, and 8.4 for reference.)

5. Infant Care Demonstrations: Take notes on others' presentations. Use your text for additional information. Submit your notes for credit.

Objectives 1, 3, and 4

6. Motor Skills of Infants and Toddlers (Chapters 8.1, 11.1, 11.2): Record a baby's motor skills sequence and match the baby's ability to a selected toy/activity. Record your work on the worksheet.

Assessments

Engagement: Participation during the unit and completion of learning activities

Knowledge: Unit quiz

Application: Newsletter article on physical development from birth to age 3.

What are three things you learned in this unit?

1. _____

2. _____

3. _____

REMEMBER

When preparing a unit work-along, include

- An assessment of prior knowledge
- An initiation or entry questions
- Unit objectives
- Learning activities
- Empty outlines for instruction or other assessment during instruction
- Assignments and related expectations or rubrics (assessment criteria can be on attached sheets)
- An opportunity for reflection
- A post-assessment

Case Studies for Analysis

As you read the following case studies, reflect on what you have learned so far and decide whether you think the teachers' practices represent defensible formative assessment. Do the teachers assess during instruction? Do they use the data gathered to make decisions about their instruction? How do they adjust content, pacing, grouping, or sequencing as a result? Are students involved in tracking their own learning, and do they receive feedback? Compare your ideas to the analysis that follows each study.

Case Study 3

Mrs. Haddon asked students in her science class to complete an empty outline on the basic properties of light. They were given the outline at the beginning of class, and they filled it in individually during class. Mrs. Haddon gave a PowerPoint presentation on the topic. Students turned their sheets in at the end of instruction. They were graded and returned prior to the unit test so students could use them to study for the final exam.

Ask yourself: Does Mrs. Haddon use assessment formatively during instruction? Does she alter her instruction based on data collected? Are students involved in tracking their learning?

Analysis: This is not an example of formative assessment. Mrs. Haddon used an empty outline, which is a formative strategy only if it's employed to gather information for the purposes of checking in on learning and adjusting instruction. Mrs. Haddon used the empty outline as a summative assessment to record performance and returned corrected papers to students. For best results, she needed to cue students when about to present information relevant to the outline. She also needed to respond formatively by giving students an opportunity to collaborate with peers to compare and discuss answers, letting students do research to find missing information, or holding conferences with students about problem areas on the outline. After students corrected and completed their outlines (either through peer sharing or teacher direction), Mrs. Haddon could then follow up with an in-class post-assessment and use feedback from that to reteach or review. Students could keep the outlines and use them as a study guide for a unit test.

Case Study 4

Teachers at Town Middle School used a schoolwide research project format with an accompanying rubric. For the first step, students selected a topic within the unit they were studying and explained what they knew about it and what they wanted to learn about it. They posted a summary of their ideas on a unit graffiti wall, where the whole class had an opportunity to discuss the topics, make suggestions, and ask any additional questions. All students then had an opportunity to revise their topic choice.

Once the teacher approved all students' selected topics, the students explained how they planned to proceed with their research (a modified K-W-L). At this point, the teacher made suggestions, based on each student's interests and abilities, on how the student might focus and narrow the project. Students then finalized their topic choice and wrote three questions that would serve as their research guide. The teacher reviewed these questions for alignment and compliance with project guidelines.

The students' next step was to identify relevant and appropriate project resources. When the class first went to the media center, some students were ready to start their search, while others received additional help with writing their questions or reviewing the research project format. Students then submitted their three preliminary resources for the teacher's approval.

This process continued with each step of the project. The teacher monitored student research skills, provided interventions, and made accommodations as needed. Feedback and assistance were always available. Some teachers at Town Middle School had students keep a research log as a place to record progress, thoughts, and questions for teacher review and response.

The school's common research project rubric covered four standards—content, organization, research skills, and product—and each standard was clarified with descriptors of four levels of mastery. At each step of the process, students self-assessed their work and then submitted both the rubric and their work-in-progress to the teacher. The alignment between the student's and the teacher's rating informed the teacher's formative response: some students got the green light to go ahead, while others were grouped for a demonstration of Web site analysis, and still others had an individual consultation with the teacher. The teachers at Town Middle School saw this model as a way to ensure there were no surprises for the students or teacher at the completion of the project.

Ask yourself: Is this a good model of formative assessment? What specific examples of formative assessment do you see embedded in the assignment?

Analysis: There is lots of formative assessment embedded in this case study. There were group and individual pre-assessments in the Graffiti Wall activity and in the K-W-L. During the project, the teacher monitored student readiness and progress, providing additional support as needed at various steps in the process. The research log was another source of formative assessment data, and the schoolwide use of the rubric made for a consistent approach to project assessment. It's notable that this rubric was not content based but, rather, focused on "21st-century" skills.

CHAPTER 5

Formative Assessment After Instruction

We all know Yogi Berra's famous phrase, "It ain't over till it's over." In the traditional classroom, when instruction is over, it *is* over. And after a hurried common review, the summative test gives the final verdict on student achievement. With formative assessment, though, when instruction is complete, teachers have one more opportunity to help students cross the finish line and meet learning goals.

The Value of Post-Instruction Assessment

Teachers today are regularly asked to account for their students' learning. In the formative classroom, this accounting occurs throughout the instructional process, from lesson planning and pre-assessment to summative assessment and standardized tests. However, assessing for learning is particularly relevant at the end of a period of instruction.

Insight into Remaining Gaps in Understanding

Granted, students are in the home stretch. At this point, there isn't time to restart the race from the beginning. But if a teacher has used formative assessment before and during instruction and has been responding instructionally to data gathered, students should not be too far behind. This last assessment will identify areas in which students could use a bit more clarification, practice, or reinforcement before a summative assessment, whether it is a standardized or teacher-created test, a final submission of student work, or the assignment of a grade.

For example, Mrs. Zakari is fairly confident that the students in her math class understand the strategies for converting data in a table into graphs. During instruction, she has used numerous examples, frequently checked for understanding, and reviewed the practice problems. But when she reviews her "one last assessment," requiring students to apply the strategies they've just learned, she is aghast to discover that a large number of students are unable to solve a real-life problem similar to one that will be on the unit test. Mrs. Zakari opens class the next day with a Bump in the Road activity. Through it, she uncovers lingering, widespread confusion about the meaning of different segments in pie charts and bar graphs.

Guidance on Final Interventions

Post-instruction assessment data help teachers select final, customized interventions to support student learning in identified trouble spots. We can see this targeted instruction in action in Mrs. Zakari's class. After discovering the students' weak spot, Mrs. Zakari gives some thought to why they might be struggling with this aspect of the curriculum. She also seeks input from her colleagues: Have they ever had a similar problem? How did they respond? Mrs. Zakari's fellow teachers share some Web sites that they have used as resources, and one offers a workbook with more examples and practice problems.

The best answer comes from a colleague who recommends a guided activity in which students create real-world problems for a whole-class review. The challenge of constructing problems focuses students on specific lesson components, including how to transfer data into various graphic representations, and Mrs. Zakari is able to offer one-on-one guidance and address specific gaps in understanding. And so, prior to giving the summative unit test, Mrs. Zakari is able to reteach the main ideas of bar graphs and pie charts—this time using a PowerPoint presentation featuring embedded student-generated problems. Her adjusted instruction incorporates more examples and provides additional, targeted practice.

One More Set of Data for Charting Growth

A validation of learning progress can be as strong an indicator of achievement as the results of any summative test; it's not just what students now know that matters, but how much progress they have made. As teachers look to final grading, the question arises as to how much formative assessments should "count." As I said earlier, this will be up to the teacher. Considerations include growth in learning versus final level of achievement and quality of work versus quality of peer and self-assessment and reflection.

I think most teachers would agree that it is unfair to use one summative measure to determine a grade when students have demonstrated proficiency in other ways. This is especially true for learners who experience intense test anxiety. Under the stress of a test, these students go into flight-or-fight mode, releasing neurotransmitters that block logical thinking. As one student explained to me, he did poorly in math not because he didn't understand the concepts but because he got too stressed out during tests. He did all his homework, participated in class discussions, and demonstrated learning during class, but his test scores never reflected his learning. For these students, factoring in formative assessment ensures that grades reflect a truer picture of what they know.

Opportunity to Reflect on Learning

Student reflection can be part of the post-instruction formative assessment of writing, presentations, products, problem-solving techniques, and portfolios. It leads to numerous positive outcomes, including increased engagement and the development of critical-thinking skills, such as analysis and evaluation.

The effectiveness of this student reflection and self-assessment depends on the teacher's providing clear guidelines on the purpose of the activity or project to be evaluated and identifying the critical content students should focus on. To accurately judge their own performance, students need to be able to measure it against set criteria, such as the content of a rubric. They do even better when they have exemplars of work at various levels of quality. Asking students to identify strategies that they can use or steps they can take to improve the quality of their work is another beneficial strategy that supports learning.

Use formative assessment after instruction to

- Identify remaining gaps in students' knowledge, skills, or understanding
  - Determine the selection of final customized interventions
  - Gain insight into the learning that has occurred
  - Provide opportunities for thoughtful reflection

In this chapter, we will look at some strategies for post-instruction formative assessment and examples of teacher practice. These will include strategies that encourage summarization and review of learning to find weak spots before summative assessment or testing. We will also discuss peer and self-assessment and how to support students' efforts to monitor their learning, set personal goals, and evaluate their own work.

Strategies for Post-Instruction Summary and Review

Most teachers do review students' learning before a summative test, but traditionally the review is the same for all students, the time allotted for review is short, and the review is not necessarily aligned with the learning goals and test. In a formative classroom, learning is regularly compared to goals, and instruction is adjusted accordingly. This is especially true of post-instruction assessment, when it is particularly important that assessment, standards, and summative measures align.

Post-instruction formative assessment strategies often incorporate summarizing, matching questions and answers, and writing questions. Teachers can even assess learning using an item from the test itself, providing that it's an item requiring students to apply, synthesize, or use other higher-order thinking skills. Some teachers might balk at this practice, but if we are asking students to show their learning, giving them support and time to prepare only strengthens their ability to demonstrate what they can do. Making post-instruction formative assessment as much like the summative test as possible will also help students with test anxiety because the test will be familiar. Based on results of the assessment, teachers can adjust whole-class instruction or customize their efforts to meet individual student needs.

Here is a closer look at some of the strategies.

Nutshelling

Summarizing is more complicated than recalling knowledge. Students must analytically select the main ideas and organize learning into a cohesive synopsis, which helps them to see the big picture. It is an important way to differentiate core concepts from inconsequential information, and it reveals a lot about students' understanding.

In Nutshelling, a teacher asks students to reflect on their learning and come up with a brief summary statement that captures the essence of it. Nutshells don't have to be written. Students might nutshell the plot of a book by drawing an illustration or by acting it out in a three-minute performance (an approach with the added benefit of movement). Mix up modes of Nutshelling to find what most engages your students.

In practice: When Mr. Perkins introduces the main concepts of the solar system to his 9th grade astronomy students, he has them create a simple web diagram with the sun in the center, surrounded by planets and information about those planets (e.g., distance from the sun, time to complete a full revolution around the sun). At the end of the unit, Mr. Perkins asks the students to expand that web to include nutshells of the unit's main ideas—density, gravity, size, and rotation—as they relate to each planet in the system. In the first diagram, at the introductory level, the sun is at the center of the web, and in the summarizing graphic, each planet is the center of its own web, with planetary details as offshoots.

When students have completed their second webs, Mr. Perkins calls on individuals to provide a nutshell report of individual planets. Each holds up his or her summary web and states facts about one planet's size, gravity, density, and location. As individuals report out, Mr. Perkins prompts the rest of the class to compare one or more of the qualities of the newly nutshelled planet with the qualities of a previously nutshelled planet.

With this post-instruction assessment, the teacher is trying to gauge the students' understanding of a complex system characterized by numerous interacting forces. The assessment reveals which students are still at the stage of acquiring knowledge about the planets and which understand the bigger picture of systems theory.

The activity also generates an additional set of formative data and a secondary outcome. Listening to student comments and questions during the activity, Mr. Perkins realizes that his instructional strategy of having students create two webs, one within the other, left them confused as to which information went into each web. He makes a note to himself that next time, he should teach each objective (solar systems versus planetary characteristics) separately. He also goes on to adjust his summative assessment so that each objective is clearly delineated into distinct parts. The new plan is to use selected-choice questions for objectives related to the universe and completion questions for objectives related to planets.

3-2-1

This strategy combines several levels of assessment. Students respond to three prompts. To the first prompt, they give three answers; to the second, two answers; and to the third, one answer—thus the name 3-2-1. The three answers could be vocabulary words or key facts from the unit. The two answers might be lingering questions or big ideas, and the one could be a question to ask another student or a way to apply new learning.

In practice: To prepare for a unit geography test, Ms. Isaacs uses 3-2-1 to ask students to identify three southern states, two major cultural influences on these states, and one way the southern states use natural resources in an economic context. These questions align with the unit test. As students name the three states, Ms. Isaacs prompts the class to provide more specific information, probing various students to gauge if they have mastered the content and then providing a bit of additional review for those she believes could benefit from it. As in Mr. Perkins's class, the students here are at different levels of knowing and understanding. Ms. Isaacs's short-answer summative test contains content similar to what she is covering in her review. Some questions focus on basic recall of knowledge, and others require students to apply knowledge to particular economic scenarios.

Across the hall from Ms. Isaacs's room, students in Mrs. Ordonez's health class complete a 3-2-1 at the end of a unit on nutrients. They select a nutrient and then explain three facts about it, describe two of its functions, and create one review question. As the review is taking place, Mrs. Ordonez offers clarification on the information students present. After noticing several inaccurate review questions related to nutrition facts, she decides, on the spot, to create a chart on the SMART Board that mirrors the one students had previously completed in class. As students continue to report out on their 3-2-1, she makes sure that what she is posting will reinforce the information that will be covered on the unit test.

Ball Toss

Ball Toss is an oral question-and-answer strategy. Because it puts students on the spot to a certain degree, teachers do need to be sensitive and cautious about potential embarrassment.

To start the activity, the teacher can pick a student's name from a hat, toss that student a ball, and ask that student a question at a level that matches his or her demonstrated knowledge and understanding. The student has the option of answering or tossing the ball to another person. If a student answers the question, the teacher can move on to the next question, or the response can be discussed for further clarification. If several students in a row pass on the ball without answering the question, the teacher knows that there are gaps in knowledge and can use that discovery as an opportunity for further review.

In practice: When Mr. Perkins uses Ball Toss to assess learning before a unit test on Earth's rotation and revolution, he notes that some students are still confusing the two concepts. He asks for volunteers to demonstrate the difference between planetary rotation and revolution and soon has all the students laughing as they spin and rotate around one another.

Q&A Mix-Up

Here, students write questions and corresponding answers about a unit of study on separate cards. The teacher checks the accuracy of answers and then randomly distributes just the answer cards, leaving each student with his or her question and someone else's answer. With the groundwork laid, a volunteer begins by asking his question. All students look at their answer cards, and those students who think they have the answer raise their cards. The teacher calls on these students, who read their answers for affirmation and, if necessary, for correction or clarification. The student holding up the correct answer gets to read his or her question next. Questions that students are unable to match indicate topics for further instruction or practice.

Student-generated questions have the advantage of serving as summary assessment, requiring students to review and sort all the learning they've acquired during the unit. Writing the questions also engages the students in the activity. Alternatively, teachers can write their own questions and answers to use in the mix-up. Although this variation offers the opportunity to closely align questions and answers with the standards and summative test, there is less student ownership. I recommend mixing up the two approaches by using some teacher-generated Q&As with many student-generated ones.

A variation of Q&A Mix-Up called Inside-Outside Circles involves arranging students in two circles, one inside the other, with students in the inner and outer rings facing one another. The questions and answers, which can be student or teacher generated, are on the same card. Students facing each other ask their questions. Then the circles move, and students face a new partner and ask their questions again. Students who don't know the correct answer need only reveal this to one other person, so while their responses are known, they are minimally public, and each student keeps track of the number of incorrect responses given to his or her questions. After students have made a full revolution, the teacher finds out which questions were the most frequently missed to determine gaps in understanding that should be addressed.

In practice: In his physical education class, Mr. Dolatz's students are finishing a unit on aerobics and cardiovascular fitness. He asks them to write questions about the unit material on white cards and the answers on blue cards. While students write, Mr. Dolatz circulates to review students' work and provide assistance and clarification. He has also prepared his own set of questions and answers, and when he's collected and quickly reviewed the students' sets, he adds a few from his set, which address vital points the students' cards have not covered.

Mr. Dolatz mixes up all the Q&A cards and redistributes them randomly. Next, he divides the class into groups of four, after which individual students take turns reading their question cards to the entire class. As each question is asked, any student who thinks he or she has the matching answer card holds it up. Students may confer with the other members of their group before holding up their cards.

Based on the quality of students' Q&A cards and their ready responses during the activity, Mr. Dolatz concludes that they have a good understanding of the subject matter in question (the relationship between aerobics and cardiovascular fitness). However, because few of the student-written questions or answers incorporated vocabulary introduced during the unit—words such as *anaerobic* and *glycogen*—he is careful to verbally reinforce these key terms throughout the rest of the review.

Grab Bag

Grab Bag is another type of review that can be based on teacher-generated or student-generated material. Simple paper lunch bags and pieces of paper are all that are needed. Each student reaches into the bag and draws a slip of paper, on which is written a question, an answer, a bit of information related to the lesson (e.g., a name, a concept, a fact), or any combination of these. Students take turns responding to their draw by answering the question (or providing the answer, *Jeopardy*-style), finding the corresponding answer to his or her question, or explaining the significance of the lesson-related information. Grab Bag can also be used for vocabulary review, with words and definitions for students to draw and match.

In practice: Ms. Ruff uses the Grab Bag strategy in her psychology class to review famous theorists. She prints brief descriptions of major theories, cuts them into sentence- and phrase-length portions, and puts the various pieces into paper bags—one cut-up theory per bag. She distributes the bags to small groups, tells each group the name of its theorist, and then asks the groups to reassemble the mixed-up pieces of their write-up and explain the theory to the rest of the class. This activity is a variation of a similar but simpler Grab Bag Ms. Ruff has done in the past, in which she put the names of different theories and theorists in a central bag and asked each student to draw a slip of paper and explain the main ideas of the theory or theorist selected.

Appendix B describes additional post-instruction assessment strategies, including A-B-C Summaries, in which students use letters of the alphabet to summarize key points, and Exit Slips, which involves students answering a question or describing their primary learning at the end of class. Various kinds of graphic organizers also make good tools for reviewing. Teachers can jumble the elements and ask students to reconstruct the content.

As you look at these suggestions for assessing after instruction in various content areas, think about how teachers might use student responses to inform further instruction.

- *Social Studies:* Write down three facts about Eleanor Roosevelt, two significant contributions she made, and one ongoing controversy about her.
- *English:* Paraphrase the author's main idea into one sentence or extract one line from a paragraph that reflects the main idea.
- *Health:* Nutshell the best ways to prevent the spread of sexually transmitted infections and diseases.
- *Physics:* Write a formula on one card and an application of it on another. We will mix up all the formulas and applications, pass them out, and have you find the match to your card.
- *World Language:* Create a flash card every day about that lesson's learning. At the end of the unit, you will use them collectively to quiz one another.
- *Driver's Ed:* When I hold up a card with a road sign, if you think you have the card with what it means on it, hold it up.

Your turn: Think about your own curriculum. How might you use summary or review strategies to assess for understanding after instruction? What might the activities tell you about student learning? How might you respond instructionally to the information generated?

Responding Instructionally

The summary and review assessment strategies discussed here are designed to help you pinpoint gaps in student knowledge, skills, or understanding so that you can plan a response that targets these specific areas. It may entail addressing confusing spots in learning, with interventions for either the whole class or individuals. You may discover students have a range of problem areas and decide to group them for differentiated intervention according to what they found most challenging to master. Use these three key questions to guide instructional responses at this stage of the process:

1. Based on the data gathered, what level of knowledge or skills do students demonstrate?

2. What level of understanding would constitute mastery sufficient for students to move on to the next lesson or unit of instruction?

3. What instructional response—utilizing both classroom strategies and school-based resources—would be best suited to bring all students to the necessary level of understanding?

Here is an example of one such response. At the conclusion of a unit on punctuation, Mrs. Chavez finds that in her 2nd period language arts class, most students are having trouble distinguishing among the uses of commas, semicolons, and colons. She responds by reteaching just those concepts, this time using a different learning activity focused on those three punctuation marks. In 3rd period language arts, post-instruction assessment indicates that students have a variety of gaps in their understanding. There, she groups students based on what they found most challenging—verb tense, adjectives versus adverbs, metaphors and similes—and provides mini-lessons and specific practice activities.

As always, when adjusting instruction based on formative assessment results, it is important to remember to try a different approach. Use a new activity, source, or different content to teach the concept. Instead of a lecture, try a WebQuest; instead of a poster, use questioning; and instead of a teacher-led review, consider having students review material in pairs. The point is to change methods and avoid teaching the material in the same way you did the first time.

Finally, you always have the option of changing the summative assessment. For example, you might resequence your planned summative test so that the concepts you've identified as the most challenging will appear at the test's end. This is a way to help students to maintain confidence and avoid discouragement. It increases the odds that the test will support a valid conclusion about what students know and can do. After all, the point of a summative assessment is to get the most accurate measure of student learning; if a frustrated student gives up halfway through and doesn't even attempt to respond to the remaining questions, you're left to wonder if he or she did or did not understand the material those questions addressed. You don't have assessment data to support either conclusion. Other options to consider include assigning different weights to different portions of the test, depending on the student, and deciding not to penalize students for not answering every question.

For example, the summative test at the end of Ms. Levar's unit on supply and demand begins with questions about basic facts, moves on to questions about the effects of supply and demand on the economy, and concludes with problems that require students to analyze and respond to data and graphs. Thanks to her ongoing formative assessment activities, Ms. Levar has a good idea of where each student stands in his or her understanding of the subject matter, and she assigns questions beyond that level less weight in scoring. This individualized scoring takes additional time, but Ms. Levar values the balance of achievement and progress that the resulting grade reflects.

Another strategy for modifying assessment is to ask students to explain their reasoning when answering questions. This allows adjustment for individuals, providing challenge at the right level for each student. For example, in answer to the prompt, "Explain how supply and demand may have far-reaching effects on the economy," two students, Vera and Stella, both of whom have demonstrated different levels of understanding, can provide appropriate answers. Based on previous assessments, Ms. Levar will give Vera full credit if she explains how supply and demand affects consumer spending, but Stella will receive full credit only if she stretches to make more complex connections between supply and demand and the workplace and the global economy. This practice ensures that a student who starts a class near mastery level continues to learn.

Allowing students some control over how they demonstrate learning gives them a better chance of showing teachers all they know. Choice in assessment is more relevant to a product or authentic type of assessment that asks students to do something with their knowledge than it is to a traditional test. Allowing students to choose whether they want to show their understanding of DNA by creating a poster or a PowerPoint presentation, making a model, acting out principles, or writing a song increases their engagement. Teachers can assess a variety of products with the same general criteria, maybe in rubric form, or students can assess the work themselves.

Peer and Self-Assessment

To be successful in the workplace, students will need the critical-thinking skills of being able to effectively assess their own work and the work of others. These skills take time to teach and learn, and secondary schools are the ideal environment in which to do so. As the brain's frontal cortex completes its development, executive function emerges and matures, and students' analytical and comparative thinking improves. At this age, students also become more adept at devising strategies to meet the challenges of monitoring and improving learning. Students' brains are developing the intellectual capacity to understand and use peer and self-assessment.

Research and Rationale

Emerging research on the value of peer and self-assessment is showing great promise. Although protocols for using it in a way that produces results that are both valid and reliable are still in the developmental stages, we do have enough information and sufficient exemplars and case studies to argue for adopting it as part of formative assessment. A meta-analysis by Sebba and colleagues (2008) confirmed that peer and self-assessments have a positive effect on learning across content areas and that students who engage in it show greater engagement in learning and increased independent learning. They are more aware of goals and objectives and have a better understanding of what they have to do to succeed.

I include peer and self-assessment in this chapter on post-instruction assessing for two reasons. First, generally it is not until instruction is complete that students understand a content standard well enough to accurately assess their standard-related learning or the standard-related learning of their classmates. Second, students typically need a great deal of practice and guidance in assessment before they are able to meaningfully evaluate their own learning or the learning of their peers.

Guidelines for Preparing Students

Teachers can offer opportunities to develop self- and peer assessment skills throughout instruction, with the goal that students may be able to assess final work. Let's look at some things to keep in mind while preparing students to assess themselves and one another.

Identify your purpose in using peer or self-assessment. Having a clear purpose for using peer and self-assessment is paramount. Teachers should ask themselves what their goal is in asking students to assess. Is it simply to have students reflect on what they or others have learned? Is it to help students move toward objectively assessing their progress toward achieving standards? Is it for students to identify and plan ways to improve their own work, or is it for a group of students to work together to achieve goals? Teachers must identify the goal for peer and self-assessment in order to choose a strategy that aligns with that objective.

Establish clear assessment criteria, and share these with students early on. To evaluate how well their work or learning meets standards or set expectations, students first need to understand the criteria. Teachers can show students examples of high-quality work and discuss what attributes make it exemplary. They can also show students lower-quality work and invite them to name ways in which it does not meet expectations. Introducing and posting exemplars at the beginning of instruction provides models against which students can measure their progressing and final work.

Rubrics are another way to document expectations. Usually presented in a table format, rubrics define standards and describe the various levels of achievement that represent progress toward those goals. Teachers can create a unit, project, or activity rubric themselves or invite students to participate in rubric creation. However, students must have access to the criteria before actual work begins so that they may set goals and assess their progress.

Give students opportunities to practice constructive feedback. When students critique one another's work, their comments should be constructive and actionable, and they should provide evidence for evaluative comments. For example, contrast "I like your poster," which does not contain helpful evidence from the work or product, with "The layout of your poster helped me understand the sequence of photosynthesis," which explains what about the poster is successful. Students' recommendations should also be specific: "I think your argument about global warming would be more convincing if you included more than one cause." The evaluator must provide comments that can be supported by the evidence of the product. If students say they didn't like the way the actor in the play read her lines, they must be able to defend that in terms of what high-quality acting looks like.

Typically, it takes students some time to develop these skills. Teachers can model giving effective feedback and provide opportunities for students to practice to prepare them for post-instruction assessments.

Tools and Strategies for Peer and Self-Assessment

Strategies for peer and self-assessment should match a teacher's goals. If reflection on learning is the goal, strategies like Muddiest Point, Exit Slips, or Journaling may be good choices. For peer feedback, Stars and Wishes works well, and for impartial measuring of products against goals, a rubric will help keep assessment and progress on track. Here is a sampling of approaches you might try.

Muddiest Point

In a Muddiest Point activity, students are asked to think about what they don't understand. This is reverse thinking—like reverse psychology—and it helps pinpoint areas of misunderstanding in material that has been previously taught. Muddiest Point can be done in large or small groups, but its effectiveness relies on students' willingness to be candid, so asking everyone to identify their muddiest point in writing and submit it anonymously can sometimes be the best approach. When submissions are anonymous, the teacher addresses all the muddiest points for the whole class and then invites anyone who would like further clarification to arrange for a private, one-on-one review.

In practice: During Mr. Pele's lesson on verb conjugations, he notices multiple muddiest point cards about the difference between the past perfect case and the past imperfect case. He uses a quick signaling activity to create small, mixed-readiness groups combining students who feel they understand and students who are less certain. The members of each group work collaboratively to generate a definition and an example of each verb case. To check students' comprehension, Mr. Pele asks each group to report out on its collective muddiest point. He repeats this with other common muddiest points to pinpoint and address specific misunderstandings.

Journaling

Journaling can be an opportunity for a more private interchange between student and teacher. Students can reflect on content in a free flow of ideas or in response to a specific prompt designed to elicit information related to the student's mastery of objectives or status related to desired learning outcomes.

In practice: In Mrs. Giani's senior project, the problem-solving process is the subject of a discrete lesson taught early in the course. After a mini-lecture on the steps to problem solving, Mrs. Giani gives her students a real-life problem to solve—actually, a problem facing adolescent characters on a popular TV show, which she illustrates by showing a snippet of the program. After watching the video, the students start on a Think–Pair–Share activity. All seems to be going well in terms of student understanding. As a final step, Mrs. Giani asks students to respond to these questions in their journal:

1. What is unclear to you about the problem-solving process?
2. When have you used it in your own life?
3. How do you think it relates to your senior project?

In Doug's journal response, he indicates that he understands the process but doesn't see a connection to his work. This is troubling to Mrs. Giani, because in her experience, connecting problem solving to the project content is essential to the project's long-term success. Rather than reteaching this point to the whole class, Mrs. Giani meets with Doug individually to talk about his areas of confusion and misunderstanding. They agree to revisit the problem-solving process over the course of Doug's project work so that she can help him navigate through any problems.

Critiques

Critiques can take a variety of forms: self or peer, formal or informal, written or oral. The biggest challenge for students is to maintain an objective perspective and provide feedback that is constructive. Critiques can work in a range of content areas and topics. They can be used in science class to examine lab work; in a culinary lab to evaluate a product; or in English class, as in the case below, to provide feedback on writing.

In practice: Early in the year in Miss Agosta's English class, it was common for students to give peer feedback about writing assignments that did not show much analysis or evaluation, such as, "It was easy to read." As Miss Agosta continues to teach her students explicit strategies for critiquing, showing them exemplars of higher- and lower-quality work and providing feedback on their assessment of others' work, their ability to peer assess improves, and their comments become more sophisticated, more attuned to writing structures and elements, and more closely aligned with the standards. For example, a student who began the year commenting, "I liked your story," was now noting, "The opening sentence grabbed my attention because of the image it created." Another student who once commented that she found a story "confusing" could now say why: "It wasn't always clear how old the hero was or where the action was taking place as the story unfolded."

Stars and Wishes

Feedback should include positive and practical comments. In Stars and Wishes, students identify two positive things about another's work and one wish for improvement. This strategy encourages students to find important points, relevant facts, and support for viewpoints while also giving constructive ideas for improving the product.

In practice: After students submitted their final science projects, Mrs. Jones held a walkabout for peer assessment. She placed a list of evaluative criteria by each project—topic clarity and focus, depth of content, organization/sequencing of the information, and project format/design—and asked students to think about the criteria and leave anonymous written feedback on each project in the format of two stars and one wish. After the walkabout, each student had a list of very positive specific comments (stars) and suggestions for improvement (wishes).

The criteria that Mrs. Jones provided were components of an ongoing assessment process her students were engaged in. For this assignment, she'd selected specific components that aligned well with the project requirements and that had been used to evaluate the first draft of their science project. After the Stars and Wishes walkabout, Mrs. Jones gave her students an opportunity to grade their own projects, based on the criteria and their peers' feedback. She took all these data into consideration when determining a summative grade for the final science project.

Rubrics

Rubrics exemplify one of the primary ideas of formative assessment: in planning assessment, you should have the end goals in mind. Rubrics provide a structure for laying out goals for students and the path to achieving them from the start of the learning process or product all the way through to its finish. They can be used to evaluate content, context, products, and performances; to provide feedback; and to support instructional decisions and judge instructional effectiveness.

Rubrics vary in format, but a rubric is essentially a scaled scoring guide with evaluative criteria that define performance standards. The criteria describe a range of acceptable and unacceptable products. The basic structure for a rubric looks like the one in Figure 5.1. Four levels of achievement are recommended. They can be given numbers or names such as *proficient, emerging,* or *developing*. The number of standards can vary to meet the particular needs of the assignment. Teachers can weight each standard in the scoring column. Student reflection and teacher comments can identify areas of strength, document growth, and provide suggestions for improvement.

FIGURE 5.1	Sample Rubric Showing Standards From Two Content Areas				
Assignment:					
	Exceeds Standard	**Meets Standard**	**Working Toward Standard**	**Below Standard**	**Weight/Score**
Language Arts Standard 1: Writing style	Engages target audience. Exemplary use of tone, sentence variety, and word choice.	Uses appropriate tone, sentence variety, and word choice for target audience.	Does not maintain appropriate tone for target audience. Sentence variety and word choice are limited.	Word choice and sentence variety do not address target audience.	/
Geology Standard 2: Problem solving using data	Critically interprets data to determine a valid solution with supporting evidence.	Analyzes appropriate data and arrives at probable solutions with supporting evidence.	Shows difficulty analyzing data and may not arrive at a solution with supporting data.	Misinterprets data and does not arrive at a solution supported by evidence.	/
Student Reflection:					**TOTAL**
Teacher Comments:					

Teachers should distribute or create rubrics with students at the beginning of instruction so that everyone will know the expectations and grading criteria from the start. Rubrics make an excellent tool for feedback during work on an assignment or project. Teachers and students can review rubrics together and compare students' work to descriptors to determine areas that need improvement. The criteria provide guidance for revisions. As a formative strategy at the end of instruction, rubrics explain the rationale for a score or grade and show progress made based on clear and objective standards. Teachers usually discover that the more students use a rubric, the more their assessment of work aligns with the teacher's. With rubrics serving as guideposts, students improve in their ability to peer and self-assess.

In practice: Mrs. Whaley has noticed that when she and her culinary students use the same checklists to assess their labs, they generally give themselves perfect scores and ignore the errors that she's careful to point out: not following the recipe, measuring incorrectly, not fully cleaning up, and so on. Based on this inconsistency between her scores and the students' scores, she decides to replace the checklist with a rubric that will include more specific details and quality indicators. Over the next few weeks she tries three different lab rubrics, each time reviewing the alignment of her scores with her students' scores and then giving both sets of scores to student groups for them to compare and contrast. They identify areas where there is misalignment and explain why they think this happened.

Ultimately, this student feedback helps Mrs. Whaley create a better-quality rubric that measures the important components of the culinary lab and is written so that everyone can understand the criteria at each level. Figure 5.2 shows the final version of their jointly created rubric. Thanks to the transparency in the creation of the rubric, both the students and the teacher clearly understand the justifications for various ratings.

Mrs. Whaley goes on to use this new rubric for several labs. Each time that students receive a score less than 3 (the cut point she has decided on), she asks them to complete a reflection on what worked well and what needed improvement. Over time, Mrs. Whaley notes that her students are becoming more proficient and realistic in their self-evaluation. She sees

FIGURE **5.2** Sample Rubric for Culinary Lab

GROUP _____ NAME(S) _____

PART 1: THE PROCESS. Includes safety, sanitation, following the recipe, timing, and community behavior.

STANDARD	EXCEEDS STANDARD 4 = A+ 3.8 = A 3.6 = A−	MEETS STANDARD 3.5 = B+ 3.4 = B 3.2 = B−	WORKING TOWARD STANDARD 3.1 = C+ 3 = C 2.8 = C−	BELOW STANDARD 2.7 = D+ 2.6 = D 2.4 = D−	Check Off	RATING
Safety/Start-up: Personal hygiene and safety rules	Exemplary personal hygiene skills. Superior compliance with safety rules.	Compliance with classroom standards for health and safety.	Needs occasional reminders about safety, cleanliness, and standards.	Neglects to comply with explicit hygiene and safety expectations.	__ Hair back __ Hands washed __ Safe practices	
Recipe & Time	Precise conformity to recipe. Feasible time plan, fully adhered to.	Recipe followed. Acceptable use of time/ planning with no major errors.	Limited application of scheduling. Recipe procedures reduced quality of product.	Time was wasted. Recipe was not followed, resulting in inferior product.	__ Follows steps __ Feasible time plan __ Good use of time	
Accuracy: Ingredients and equipment	Exemplary selection and use of ingredients. Accurate and careful use of equipment and supplies.	Appropriate use of equipment and supplies. Accurate use of ingredients, measuring, mixing, and sequencing.	Some confusion about equipment and/or supplies. Minor errors in use of ingredients and following the recipe.	Significant number of errors or careless use of equipment and supplies. Difficulty in using ingredients and following recipe.	__ Measured accurately __ Mixed correctly __ Used proper equipment	
Community Behavior: Respect, responsibility, and participation	Group worked well together, respects differences, and collaborates responsibly in lab. Supports/ encourages this in others.	Satisfactory level of respect, responsibility, and participation contributed to an efficient lab.	Disagreements and inequitable sharing of responsibilities resulted in frustration/conflict. Inconsistent adherence to rules.	Group had difficulty working together, sharing duties, and respecting differences. Disregard for rules and rights of others.	__ Teamwork __ Everyone contributes __ Respectful	
Cleanup	All areas were completely clean and sanitized.	Most areas were clean and sanitized. Most steps completed.	As noted, some steps missed.	Inadequate cleanup. Work area was not ready for next group.	__ Supplies returned __ Dishes clean, dry __ Stove clean/off __ Sink clean, dry __ Counter sanitized __ Floor swept	
Comments:					Subtotal:	

(Continued)

FIGURE 5.2	Sample Rubric for Culinary Lab (continued)

PART 2: PRODUCT and PRESENTATION. Includes recipe selection, appearance, palatability, presentation.

STANDARD	EXCEEDS STANDARD $4 = A+$ $3.8 = A$ $3.6 = A-$	MEETS STANDARD $3.5 = B+$ $3.4 = B$ $3.2 = B-$	WORKING TOWARD STANDARD $3.1 = C+$ $3 = C$ $2.8 = C-$	BELOW STANDARD $2.7 = D+$ $2.6 = D$ $2.4 = D-$	Check Off	RATING
Actions to Ensure Quality: Planning, recipe selection, level of challenge	Exemplary planning. Recipe fulfills requirements and is also distinctive and stretches students' abilities.	Planning was complete. Recipe meets requirements and uses routine skills.	Needs occasional reminders about safety, cleanliness, and standards.	Planning had several errors or was incomplete. Difficulty in selecting appropriate recipe.	__ Market order __ Planning sheet __ Highlighted recipe __ Reserved items	
Finished Product: Aligns with picture/ recipe	Product exceeds aesthetic expectations in every aspect.	Product closely resembles picture or expected standards for color, shape, and size.	Product is similar to picture or expectations but not fully aligned.	Recipe was followed, but product didn't align with aesthetic expectations.	__ Color __ Size and shape __ Visual appeal	
Palatability: Taste, texture, edibility	Product has superior taste, texture, and edibility.	Product has the expected taste, texture, and edibility.	Product has acceptable taste or texture or edibility.	Product lacks the expected taste, texture, and edibility.	__ Taste __ Texture __ Edibility	
Service/Presentation: Plating, serving, presentation, behavior	Product was uniquely and creatively plated, served, and presented. Exceptional setting and manners.	Product was appropriately plated, served, and presented. Proper setting and manners.	Service, setting, manners, and presentation were acceptable but flawed in one area.	Product was plated and served with more than one flaw. Manners were poor. Table wasn't set.	__ Plating __ Service __ Table setting __ Manners	
Comments:					Subtotal:	

more and more alignment between student self-assessment and her own assessment of their work. As this is happening, grades also improve, due, she thinks, to students' clearer idea of learning expectations.

REFLECT AND APPLY

Here are some ideas for peer and self-assessments in different content areas. How might the teacher support students in these evaluations, and what are some possible ways students could use the assessment information?

- *Technology:* Create a storyboard for a video. Use the attached rubric to self-assess and peer assess both process and content during the development of the storyboard and for the final product.
- *Math:* Generate examples of using logic to develop hypotheses and draw conclusions, and then assess one another's ideas. Compare your answers to the flow chart discussed in class, and reflect on its similarities and differences to your work.
- *History:* How did World War II change the social and cultural conditions in the United States? Create T charts of the influence and outcome. Peer assess for accuracy of information and for adequate support for ideas. Give two stars and one wish for improvement.
- *Psychology:* Create a poster on contemporary adolescent issues for a poster competition. Note that final scores will reflect combined feedback from peer and teacher assessment, based on a collaboratively developed rubric.
- *English:* Peer review one another's persuasive essays, focusing on the use of facts and data to support the stated position. Critique for the best connection and for the least-clear muddiest point.

Your turn: How could you incorporate a peer or self-assessment strategy in your curriculum? What would be the goal for using it? How would you build students' skills in assessing and giving feedback, and how would you establish criteria? What would be the next step after the post-instruction evaluations?

Responding Instructionally

One of the primary reasons for using peer or self-assessment is having students face the decision of what to do next. Once students have accurate and constructive feedback, the next question is what to do with it. As with other formative assessments after instruction, peer and self-evaluation allows the opportunity for closing gaps before the race is over. Feedback from peers and information from rubric-based self-assessment should show students their weak areas and the steps they can take to progress toward goals. Teachers, of course, can help students use data from these evaluations to make a learning plan, suggesting alternative resources, content, or approaches.

Teachers can always group for peer assessment. Students in groups can give one another feedback and help one another plan next steps. Maintaining objectivity in light of friendships and rivalries takes time, practice, and patience; however, these are part of the skill set students will need in the real world. How to group students for peer assessment is a tricky question for teachers. Mixed-ability groups and homogeneous groups offer different advantages. In mixed groups, students have the opportunity to learn from each other. In homogeneous groups, teachers can spend more time with groups that need extra support. Each provides its own challenge to differentiation and assessment. Teachers must decide how to group based on the unique needs of each class and the outcome they have in mind for the assessment, whether it be learning to collaboratively solve problems or understanding that achievement is something definable that can be reached through constructive evaluation and measurements of success.

Case Studies for Analysis

As you read the case studies, reflect on what you have learned about using assessment after instruction. Decide whether the practices represent valid and reliable use of formative assessment. Compare your ideas to those in the analysis at the end of each study.

Case Study 5

All the Algebra I teachers at Eastville High School gave a common assessment midway through each quarter and again at the quarter's end. These tests aligned with the state goals and high school curriculum. The teachers prepared their students for the test by giving them released items from prior tests to take home and review. After students took the tests, the teachers divided the test papers among themselves for anonymous and random scoring. Several weeks after the test, the scores were distributed to each teacher. The teachers put the scores in their grade books and gave the results to their students. Some went over the test with the students and explained various answers.

Ask yourself: Did the Eastville High algebra teachers use a formative postinstruction assessment? Was their review successful in identifying gaps in learning? How did they respond instructionally to review data? What would you advise the Algebra I teachers to do differently next time?

Analysis: Although common assessments have the potential to be part of the formative assessment process, in this case, the teachers needed to assess formatively before giving the tests and use the data they gathered to target specific areas. After instruction, teachers gave students some sample problems as a review, but we didn't see teachers gathering data from these problems to identify gaps in learning. The teachers didn't customize teaching after the review to respond to differences in students' demonstrated levels of understanding of the standards tested for on the upcoming test. The school also did not use test results formatively to adjust curriculum or standards or future teaching of the unit. Teachers did not even review their own students' tests to identify areas of weakness or strength.

Formative assessment requires teachers to do something with data beyond recording scores in a grade book. These teachers need to report subscores by goal and review items that were missed by a predetermined percentage of the students. They need to reflect on their data and devise instructional responses, such as whole-class reviews, extra help sessions, or individual support. This assessment could have been more formative if teachers had done the following:

- Identified common gaps and retaught accordingly.
- Incorporated formative strategies, such as a Grab Bag, which involves solving practice problems, or Feathers and Salt, which requires students to identify areas of confidence and areas where they need more help.
- Grouped students for targeted review based on identified needs.
- Incorporated student self-assessment with feedback to the teacher, such as Exit Slips or 3-2-1.
- Incorporated student self-assessment in which students compare their achievement to standards expressed in student-friendly terms.

Case Study 6

In her health class, Mrs. Williams randomly grouped her students and asked the groups to brainstorm a list of nutshell facts from all the units they had studied so far. Each group posted and shared their ideas (typically related to drugs, alcohol, tobacco, communicable and noncommunicable diseases, and fitness) and went on to expand their individual lists based on other groups' postings. Mrs. Williams then asked her students to select one topic they found personally interesting and would like to study further. After students expressed their individual preferences, she quickly divided them into small groups. There, students created a T chart that showed what they had learned about the physical and mental health implications of their topic by putting facts such as descriptions, causes, and data on the left side of the chart and outcomes and effects on the right side. Groups then reviewed one another's work and provided feedback based on selected assessment criteria that included accuracy of facts, clarity of information, and legitimacy of effects. Mrs. Williams reviewed this feedback and added her own.

Next, Mrs. Williams asked the student groups to create a poster or brochure to advocate for lifestyle decisions that maximized lifelong health.

The final product was peer, teacher, and self-evaluated, based on a rubric providing criteria for content, organization, and motivational appeal. With the rubric scores, Mrs. Williams identified gaps in learning and provided additional resources and support as needed. She allowed students to revise their product based on this first round of feedback. The final products were both student and teacher assessed. After students received their grading sheet, they had an opportunity to reflect and respond.

Ask yourself: What information did Mrs. Williams and her students gain from assessment? Did students receive feedback opportunities to relearn or revise? How was learning progress demonstrated or measured? Did Mrs. Williams use assessment formatively throughout the case study?

Analysis: The process that Mrs. Williams used incorporated many components of formative assessment. The nutshell gave her a pre-assessment of how well students could recall prior learning from earlier units. And in the small groups, she worked more closely with those who needed more help. She diagnosed gaps through peer assessment and addressed these through feedback and reteaching before students began to work on their product. Evaluation criteria for the product were explained prior to the commencement of work, and there were opportunities for revision.

Further questions about this scenario to consider include the following:

- How was feedback on the T charts given, and what was it based on?
- How was the rubric developed, and did students have practice with it before it was used summatively?
- Was there a required cut-point on the rubric poster that influenced the opportunities for revision, or could all students make revisions?

What other questions or reflections do you have on this final case study?

PART 3

Making Connections and Furthering Change

- What is the relationship between standardized and formative assessment?
- What is formative assessment's relationship to standards-based reform and other school improvement initiatives?
- There's a great deal of buzz about 21st-century learning. How might formative assessment support those concepts?
- Where does formative assessment fit into a balanced approach to assessment?
- What can schools do to establish more balanced assessment systems?

Your turn: Take a quick scan of the chapters in this section and write two other questions that immediately come to mind.

We have looked at practical strategies for assessing before, during, and after instruction and at the options for responding instructionally to data gathered. Now you should be to ready to begin tracking and supporting your students' growth in learning. But in this closing part of the book, I would like to expand our focus to include how the practice of formative assessment supports other current educational models and theories and how classroom formative assessment can be the start of changing the culture of schools, districts, and states to make them more centered on improving students' learning.

Chapter 6 will show that formative assessment provides a way to connect several current reforms, models, and theories. Specifically, I'll focus on its essential role in supporting cognitive theory, multiple intelligences, and differentiated instruction. In Chapter 7, we'll explore how formative assessment in the classroom can serve to align the efforts of teachers, administrators, and education leaders at the school, district, state, and even national policy levels so that all are working with common useful data toward the same purpose: helping all students learn and achieve. I'll discuss organizing and reporting-in data from classroom assessments to inform not only teachers' decisions but also school and district adjustments in instruction and curricula. We'll also see how to support teachers' efforts to learn formative assessment practices and work together toward improvement.

Peter Senge (2000) describes schools as organizations that are continually learning. If so, their educators must be acting collaboratively toward a shared vision. I believe that formative assessment is the nexus for educational improvement. If we work together to incorporate it as part of a balanced system of assessment, we should be able to monitor our progress and adjust our practice to achieve maximum learning for all students, which is the goal of every educator.

CHAPTER 6

Improving Teaching and Learning Through Formative Assessment

Theories of learning are always emerging and changing. New information about how the brain works, new ideas about students' individual learning styles, new findings relating to the best conditions and atmosphere for learning, and of course, new ideas about how best to measure learning all make for new recommended practices in the classroom. It's a maze for educators at all levels: those making policy and those carrying it out.

To navigate this jumble of educational paths, I recommend that you follow the advice of a favorite professor during my doctoral studies: *take the helicopter view.* If you can expand your perspective and get a wide enough view, you can see where the paths go and choose those that will lead you to the goal of improved student learning. In this chapter, we will take a big-picture look at some current theories of learning so that we can see how formative assessment fits in. From this vantage point, it is clear that formative assessment is far more than another theory or reform to add to the already confusing mix; rather, it is a point at which many current ideas about education actually converge. It's a crossroads, so to speak, where educational routes that are based on the belief that all students can learn—just in different ways and with different outcomes and, therefore, using different strategies and different measures—all come together.

The three principle education paths we will see intersecting with formative assessment in our helicopter survey are *cognitive theory, multiple intelligences,* and *differentiated instruction.*

Cognitive Theory, the Brain, and Formative Assessment

A study of cognitive theory and related teaching practice usually starts with the work of Jean Piaget, who described the stages of children's intellectual development and proposed that cognitive abilities and schemas increase in complexity as children grow and develop. Piaget's work was based on observations of his own children and children in his community—a small population, yet his definitions and descriptions of emerging cognitive abilities have held up over time and have been supported by recent research involving imaging of the brain.

In the past 30 years or so, new medical imaging techniques, such as MRI, have begun allowing neuroscientists to measure and chart the way brains think and process information. Renate Caine and Geoffrey Caine (1991) were among the early pioneers who translated emerging research on cognition and brain function into educational applications. The three tenets below capture the Caines' primary interpretations of evidence from brain research in relation to learning.

The brain learns best when it is readied for learning. Ways to prepare the brain include

- Establishing mind-set and inclination
- Encouraging movement during learning
- Using specific strategies that are identified, learned, and practiced

The brain learns by making connections. It does this by

- Creating links to prior knowledge and experience
- Constructing new knowledge by building on prior knowledge and experience
- Generating patterns to create meaning
- Putting together parts to make wholes
- Making meaning out of new learning
- Seeking opportunities to process information in different ways

The brain learns best when specific emotional and social conditions are met. This happens when

- Content is personally meaningful
- Choice is part of learning
- Work is reasonably challenging
- Learning takes place in a positive emotional climate
- Learning involves social interaction
- Meaningful feedback is provided
- Continued positive conditions boost intrinsic motivation

Although there is more qualitative evidence than quantitative research supporting these core cognitive elements (readiness, connections, and social and emotional needs), it is difficult to argue with the main premises of cognitive theory: that mind-set is important, that each of us builds on our past experience, and that how we feel about ourselves and our learning is crucial. Let's see how formative assessment intersects with each of these three ideas.

Formative Assessment's Role in Priming the Brain

Formative assessment contributes to preparing the mind to learn. Pre-assessment serves the dual purpose of surveying students' pre-existing knowledge and initiating the lesson by engaging students and piquing their interest, helping to capture their attention and create a mind-set that anticipates learning.

Pre-assessment also can get students moving, which coincides with the cognitive premise that movement encourages learning. As we have seen, teachers can design signaling to involve students standing up, shaking fists, or moving other body parts to indicate answers. Think of how the Corners pre-assessment strategy requires students to move to the corner that matches their response to a question.

Finally, when teachers use pre-assessment strategies routinely, these strategies become a known and practiced method, an established cognitive pathway that promotes learning readiness.

Here's an example of what this looks like. In her middle school art classes, Mrs. Frye uses a combination of pre-assessment and initiation to begin each lesson, asking students to each share one example or application of the previous lesson's content. For instance, on the day after a focus on complementary colors, she begins class by taking students outside for five minutes and asking them to find and then report examples of complementary colors in nature. With this activity, Mrs. Frye gets everyone's attention, lets students move about, and is able to assess their understanding and offer clarification and correction as needed. Similarly, she begins class the day after a lesson on perspective by asking students to go into the halls and sketch some examples of perspective. In Mrs. Frye's classroom, pre-assessment has become an expected routine for her students, priming their brains for the new learning of the day and helping Mrs. Frye to increase the effectiveness of that instruction.

Formative Assessment's Role in Building Meaning

Formative assessment supports the brain in making connections by linking prior knowledge to new learning, putting together parts and wholes, and providing opportunities to process information in different ways.

When teachers use pre-assessments to gather data about students' knowledge, skills, and beliefs, they ask students to call up what they already know. This makes that information readily available for making new connections with upcoming instruction. For example, Mr. Martinez begins his

Spanish lesson with a pre-assessment for vocabulary in the form of a human bingo game. Students take a vocabulary bingo card with them as they walk around the room and ask their classmates which words they recall from a prior lesson. Following up with a quick signaling activity, Mr. Martinez can see which words were recalled frequently and which were seldom recalled. He uses these results to identify a starting point for the day's lesson.

Students experience a boost in confidence when they feel they have some knowledge of a topic at the beginning of instruction. Most learners, adults as well as children, will have a heightened sense of anxiety when confronted with a previously unknown topic. Pre-assessment provides clear learning expectations from the beginning and gives students a foundation for connecting the learning to come.

Once students make connections to prior knowledge, experience, and skills, teachers can move them up through the levels of Bloom's taxonomy (Bloom & Krathwohl, 1956). Building on and applying knowledge is the next step in generating bigger patterns, making wholes out of parts, and creating new meaning. Secondary students can be expected to identify, describe, and use their understanding to compare and explain. Moving up the ladder, teachers can ask students to apply and analyze their learning by charting and correlating. Finally, teachers should challenge students to demonstrate their ability to synthesize by evaluating and predicting and their ability to create new ideas by designing and defending. Formative assessment during instruction gives students an opportunity to display their understanding at various cognitive levels, and the information teachers gather from these assessments helps them to adjust instruction to best support students' cognitive growth.

Figure 6.1 shows how specific formative assessment strategies align with levels of Bloom's taxonomy. These strategies, which call for demonstrating knowledge using a variety of formats, including drawing, talking, acting, and writing, correlate with the Caines' conclusion that the brain requires opportunities to process information in different ways. Note that if reaching higher levels of cognition is an instructional goal, then synthesis of knowledge and the production of original products (such as newsletters or inventions) are expected. Students can use rubrics, self-assessment, and peer assessment to evaluate their work.

FIGURE 6.1	Bloom's Taxonomy and Formative Assessment	
Bloom's Taxonomy	**Application**	**Sample Formative Strategies**
Knowing	Embedding learning in memory	Give three facts Quicktalk Quickwrite
Understanding	Fitting into prior learning; considering past knowledge by comparing and explaining	Think–Pair–Share Web diagrams
Applying	Using the learning in multiple and individualized ways	Application Cards Brainstorming Journaling
Analyzing	Making meaning by exploring and questioning	Chunking Corners Continuum with support for position taken Pros and Cons
Synthesizing/Evaluating	Combining/connecting; putting ideas together; judging the ideas; critiquing	Continuum Feathers and Salt Gallery Self- and peer review Socratic questioning
Creating	Generating something new by planning and producing	Skits Cartoons Brochures Maps Quickdraw

We can see an example of using connections to support learning in Mr. Rossi's American Studies class. He distributes a work-along, which contains the unit's objectives in relation to the assignments, readings, and in-class instructional activities, and then asks his students to consider what life was like in the 1950s. After reading a collection of interviews in which people share their memories of that era, the class generates a list of icons and symbols of the time, posting them on a Gallery wall. This personalization, both individual and cultural, creates meaning for students.

Mr. Rossi continues this Gallery activity by asking students to sort the posted data by categories: entertainment, literature, styles, and world events. The teacher and students go on to address each category through selected instructional methods, including lectures, poster creation, and WebQuests. The products students create are critiqued through rubric-based self-assessment and teacher assessment. By considering parts of the culture, students begin to get a more complete picture of life in the 1950s.

The class then works to generate meaning by exploring the events of the time in relation to the influences on them. Television, suburbs, and Communism are all examined in terms of how they influenced daily life, and students work in a Think–Pair–Share to capture their insights in a T chart. These lessons provide numerous opportunities to create links, build knowledge, generate patterns, and make meaning.

Additionally, each student is allowed to personalize the learning to his or her own experience and gather information through preferred modalities. For example, during the unit, each keeps a vocabulary journal with new words (e.g., *nuclear family, beatnik, espionage*), their definitions, and an example of the words' use in context. To apply this learning, the students have the option of taking 15 vocabulary words and creating a crossword, writing a song, or writing a play. Mr. Rossi assesses this work for appropriateness and accuracy of use.

Toward the end of the unit, there is a Corners activity in which Mr. Rossi asks students to choose whether they think "life was better back then" or "life was worse back then." Students discuss among themselves why they have selected their preferred corner and elect one or two members of their group to report out on their reasoning and the support for their position. For Mr. Rossi, listening in and asking questions of his own during the presentations, the activity brings to light some misunderstandings about the difference between a cold war and a hot war and about the effect this particular Cold War had on 1950s culture. His response is to assign additional targeted readings and to ask students to submit brief written summaries, which he will review for accuracy and a sense of students' understanding.

Prior to the summative exam, which is mostly constructed-response items, Mr. Rossi employs a Grab Bag activity with icons and symbols of the 1950s. The exam also includes a reflection question in which students must compare their life today to what their life would be if it were suddenly 1953 again.

As you can see, there is a lot of formative assessment embedded throughout this unit, and it is employed to help make the subject matter meaningful.

Formative Assessment's Role in Emotional and Social Support

Even though Benjamin Bloom and David Krathwohl (1956) long ago identified the affective domain as an integral part of their taxonomy of educational objectives, many teachers still overlook the role of feelings and personal interactions in the classroom. This is especially true as standardized test preparation takes up more time in classroom instruction.

Elements of the affective domain include emotions, attitudes, and interpersonal relationships. Specific applications of this domain include attempting, contributing, valuing, sharing, and disputing. Students' willingness to learn and their belief in their ability to learn are part of their affect. Early in their schooling, and almost always by the time they reach the secondary level, students develop a strong idea of their academic abilities. Through comparison to peers and feedback from teachers, they know where they stand in the pack, and their willingness to learn something new or try a new strategy is frequently influenced by prior successes and failures. Formative assessment and its accompanying use of goal setting, scaffolding, positive feedback, and self-assessment can improve students' self-efficacy (Margolis & McCabe, 2006), thus boosting their confidence in their ability to achieve. How students feel about learning and their belief in their ability to learn lay the groundwork for successful outcomes.

Lev Vygotsky, a Russian-born psychologist, hypothesized that interpersonal relationships have a significant influence on a child's development. Children learn by following adults' examples and receiving appropriate guidance. Vygotsky maintained that as a child follows an adult's example, he or she gradually develops the ability to do certain tasks without help or assistance. He also articulated the now well-known concept of the zone of proximal development, "the distance between the actual developmental level as determined by independent problem solving and the level of potential development as determined through problem solving under adult guidance, or in collaboration with more capable peers" (1978, p. 86).

A teacher who incorporates Vygotsky's idea of the zone of proximal development sets out to provide instruction and learning activities that are neither too easy nor too difficult for the student. Formative assessment provides a sound basis for determining both this optimal degree of challenge and the supports necessary to move a student from one level of learning to the next. It helps teachers meet learners' emotional needs by providing a record of learning and useful feedback that promotes feelings of efficacy. Teachers in a formative classroom point out progress as well as deficiencies and, most importantly, offer strategies and resources for overcoming shortfalls. This personalized, nonthreatening support helps to build students' confidence in their ability to master a subject.

Consider this example. In Mrs. Pitt's Consumer Math class, problem solving is done in mixed groups as much as possible. For one assignment, she asks heterogeneous groups of three to research a car purchase using a set of criteria, requirements, and guidelines to guide their efforts. Students keep track of their progress in research logs, noting individual contributions to each step. Mrs. Pitt reviews these logs to monitor progress, and the data she gathers inform one-on-one interventions and guidance as well as positive comments and reinforcement. As the unit progresses, students have multiple opportunities to collaborate, make a contribution, share and compare information, and debate in a nonthreatening way. Mrs. Pitt provides in-class review time prior to the summative assessment, and she gives students who feel they need help developing knowledge or confidence the option of participating in an extra review session. The summative assessment itself is a problem similar to a teacher-guided analysis the class undertakes together as part of unit instruction.

This example helps to illustrate why formative assessment is such an effective way to provide learners with emotional and social support. Stiggins and Popham (2008) assert that "because assessment for learning is a particularly strong student-focused approach to instruction, an approach in which students become personally involved in monitoring and adjusting how they are attempting to learn, this achievement-enhancing strategy is almost certain to have an impact on student's affect, meaning their personal perceptions and predispositions about their learning" (p. 78). The importance of balancing cognitive and affective elements in instruction cannot be overstated.

Multiple Intelligences

Around the same time that neuroscientists began using brain imaging to explain that different brains learn in different ways, Howard Gardner (1983, 1993) was redefining educators' concept of intelligence. He proposed that each person has varying levels of seven different types of intelligence: verbal-linguistic, logical-mathematical, musical, bodily-kinesthetic, spatial, interpersonal, and intrapersonal. According to Gardner, most standardized tests measure verbal-linguistic and logical-mathematical intelligences, and most classroom instruction is focused on these same abilities. He argued that students also need to develop and express their musical, kinesthetic, spatial, and personal skills.

Critics of this theory say that there is a lack of empirical data to support Gardner's claim; however, emerging neuroscience research does support the idea that different brains learn differently. A study at the University of Pennsylvania (2009) found that visual learners, as compared to verbal learners, showed increased activity in the visual processing part of the brain. Verbal learners showed more brain activity in the verbal processing areas. There are parts of the brain that are larger or smaller, more or less active, in every child's brain (Rubenstein, 2008). At the same time, the brain is fluid, flexible, and malleable; intelligence and abilities are not fixed, and they can be altered through new learning and practice. These findings seem to indicate that providing students with opportunities to develop multiple abilities and intelligences is a reasonable course of action.

Gardner's theory of multiple intelligences has been widely embraced by educators. The theory supports most teachers' experience-based belief that individual children learn differently and have preferred learning styles. Many schools have incorporated the theory of multiple intelligences in their instruction with a great deal of success, giving students the opportunity to explore and express knowledge in ways that develop intelligences beyond just verbal-linguistic and logical-mathematical.

We can see an example in Ms. Emmons's history class. For a unit on the U.S. Civil War, she incorporates activities that require students to create a character analysis of a leading figure in the war (interpersonal); a battlefield grid and illustrations of life in the 1860s (spatial); a multimedia presentation on Gettysburg, including edited video footage of rehearsed and performed "eyewitness" reports of and reactions to the battle (kinesthetic); and war songs and lyrics (musical). There's also the example of Mrs. Scott, a math teacher who teaches the construction of geometric shapes by dividing students into small groups to work on tasks related to specific intelligences: calculations (logical-mathematical), shape construction (kinesthetic), presentation coordination (interpersonal), and project reports (verbal-linguistic). Multiple intelligences lends itself well to research projects where the overall goals, objectives, and evaluation criteria are the same for all students but the products and mode of presentation can be individually selected.

Identifying Multiple Intelligences

Formative assessment can be used to help teachers identify students' intelligences and preferred learning styles and then design instruction accordingly. The earlier in the school year that teachers assess for this information, the better. I know of one teacher who spent a year with a new grade level creating fabulous, highly effective lesson plans only to see those lessons flop with the next year's class. The first year's class had many learners with high levels of kinesthetic intelligence who thrived with hands-on activities. The following year's class had many more learners with dominant verbal-linguistic intelligence; their preferred learning style was to sit back and listen, and they found the hands-on activities frustrating. In general, teachers tend to create instruction that reflects their own dominant intelligences and preferred learning styles and the dominant intelligences and preferred learning styles of the majority of their students. However, they must be sure to also provide alternative learning opportunities and support to students who fall outside the majority.

Responding Instructionally to Multiple Intelligences

As we have seen, formative assessment strategies ask students to use a variety of formats in responding, encompassing a range of Gardner's intelligences. Figure 6.2 shows some formative strategies and the intelligence they call on. Based on the results of these assessments, teachers can choose to adjust instruction to correspond to specific intelligences and thus facilitate student learning. The results of assessment can also help in determining the format of future assessments.

Assessing Across a Range of Student Products

When students are producing different products as a result of instruction that supports multiple intelligences and varied learning styles, the question arises of how assessment can be valid and reliable. Whatever the process and product, teachers should establish consistent standards and grading criteria for all students.

In Ms. Coates's class, students are studying medieval society and learning about a range of topics, from weapons to food to women's rights. Each

FIGURE 6.2	Multiple Intelligences and Formative Assessment	
Intelligence	**Application**	**Sample Formative Strategies**
Verbal-Linguistic	Student writes it down and tells others	Minute Paper Journaling
Spatial	Chart it: format ideas related to a specific term	Empty Outlines Graphic organizers
Bodily-Kinesthetic	Demonstrate it	Model the steps Line-Up
Logical-Mathematical	Count or measure	Color-Coding Clusters
Musical	Put it to a beat	Create a rhythm haiku
Interpersonal	Group work	Muddiest Point Bump in the Road
Intrapersonal	Self-assessment	Journaling

student is required to present a different product that shows depth of learning about a particular topic, and their various products (e.g., a PowerPoint presentation about the art of Artemisia Gentileschi, a chart showing the economics of serfs and landowners, a play about apprenticing and careers, a poster about nutritional deficiencies) are all assessed based on common criteria: accuracy of content, depth of knowledge, organization of information, relevance of presentation format, and engagement of audience. Ms. Coates provides rubrics that make these criteria clear to everyone from the outset. The rubrics are also used in formative peer and self-assessments that require using interpersonal and intrapersonal intelligences.

Many teachers have heard testimonials from students about how instruction and assessments that offered the opportunity to use multiple intelligences improved their learning experience. My favorite testimonial comes from a high school senior, talking about his project. This young man, who had a flash of red hair and a minor disability, had a history of working very hard not to draw further attention to himself. His one extracurricular activity in high school was marching band, where he played the tuba and the baritone sax. For his project, he decided to write an original musical score—nothing extravagant, he told himself, just enough to get by. This did not go as planned. The project became all-consuming, and this student found himself writing an entire symphony, using MIDI technology. It was performed by the school orchestra at their final concert of the year . . . to resounding applause.

In his final reflection, he had this to say: "For four years I've been invisible at my high school. I've done what teachers asked me and haven't gotten into trouble, but my project, for the first time in my life, made me realize what I am capable of doing. I learned that I know a lot more than people think I do. People were impressed by something I thought was pretty simple. It makes me feel intelligent, in a way."

Differentiated Instruction

Since the days of the one-room schoolhouse, teachers have struggled to deliver instruction in a way that meets the needs of each of their students. Teachers are resourceful, and when they were expected to teach students from 1st through 12th grade in the same room with a blackboard and a potbelly stove, they used some of the same techniques we use today—peer learning, pacing, and scaffolding—although they wouldn't have used the same terminology.

Recently, there has been a resurgence of interest in how to teach a wide range of students in the same classroom. This interest has been driven partly by the Individuals with Disabilities Education Act (IDEA), which requires that all students, regardless of their limitation or disability, have access to the same educational opportunities as other students. In some states, special education students are mandated by law to spend 80 percent of their day in classrooms with general education students. The challenge of meeting the needs of a wide range of students in the same classroom led to the unambiguous requirement that teachers change and adapt traditional instructional strategies. Differentiated instruction is one model for how teachers can meet the challenge.

Carol Ann Tomlinson has been a leader in differentiated instruction, authoring many books and articles that offer practical guidance for teaching all students successfully in today's classrooms. In her view, differentiated instruction is a continuum of teaching and learning. It is not one strategy but, rather, an array of strategies that teachers select and use to meet the needs of individual learners. Tomlinson (2007) defines differentiated instruction with four adjectives: *responsive, intentional, fair,* and *respectful.* By *responsive,* she means that since all students differ, teachers need to respond to these individual needs. *Intentional* means that teaching is purposefully planned to ensure the maximum growth of each student. *Fair* implies that every student has what he or she needs to learn. Finally, Tomlinson uses *respectful* to mean that the individual needs are understood, and instructional strategies take these needs into account. All these splendid terms are relevant to formative assessment. We can see where the two educational paths converge in Figure 6.3.

Evidence of the effectiveness of differentiated instruction has been generalized from research on its component parts. Differentiation incorporates many other theories, including theories of cognition, multiple intelligences, motivation, and social learning. Research that supports or refutes various

FIGURE 6.3	Differentiated Instruction and Formative Assessment
Differentiated Instruction Features	**Formative Assessment Features**
Responsive to individual needs	Data are gathered to identify student needs
Teaching is planned to ensure maximum growth	Areas of requisite growth are clearly identified
Learning is guided	Student understanding is monitored
Instruction is purposefully planned	Instruction is based on students' assessed readiness and starting points in order to support learning
Each student is treated fairly	Each student gets what assessment data indicate he or she needs to progress
Teaching is designed to meet individual needs and learning style	Needs and learning style are measured through ongoing formative assessment, and instruction is customized accordingly
Content is modified	Scaffolding, tiered activities, and grouping are based on assessed needs
Learning goals are modified	Different resources and measures are used
Instruction is student focused	Peer and self-assessment inform learning

strategies for teaching gifted students, students with special needs, or diverse cultural groups is easily accessed. Research on problem solving, neurobiology, motivation, and other related topics is also readily available. And there's an adequate amount of psychological research that shows that tasks that are too easy lead to boredom and that tasks that are too hard lead to frustration, which supports the wisdom of differentiating student products of learning to be fair and respectful.

Supporting Responsive and Intentional Instruction

The first step in providing responsive instruction is knowing what you are responding to. Identifying each student's background knowledge, readiness to learn, and interest in a topic is essential. Formative assessment offers many strategies for pre-assessing for a variety of things, from factual knowledge to higher-order thinking skills to personal beliefs or dispositions to learning style. In response to this information, teachers may (1) change the content to meet the needs of the learner, (2) change the process or modality in which the child learns, and (3) adjust the expectations for products or outcomes of learning as well as the learning environment. These teacher choices are intentional, based on data, and designed to further each student's learning.

Here's an example from Ms. Miele's Environmental Studies class. After a pre-assessment and a PowerPoint presentation on definitions and descriptions of air and water pollution, she divides students into three groups based on readiness and preferred learning style. A student work-along describes goals, activities, and assessments of the unit. Miss Miele works directly with one group to ensure their understanding of key concepts such as smog, acid rain, and the ozone layer. After the students in this group create a concept map, she asks them to design a poster explaining strategies to reduce pollution. She checks in frequently and provides feedback and guidance.

The pre-assessment results and past performance of the second group of students have led Miss Miele to conclude that they have a solid mastery of the main ideas. She gives them additional articles to read that present opposing viewpoints on the problem. She then asks them to create a chart explaining strategies to combat the causes of air and water pollution and why some people or groups might be opposed to these interventions. Miss Miele reviews their summary sheet of the articles, asks them questions about their own viewpoints, and encourages them to be open-minded in reporting on the range of ideas.

The third group is composed of students who are active, hands-on learners. Miss Miele asks them to design a Web site that will inform their community of local pollution problems and solutions, and she encourages them to delve deeply into all aspects of the topic. She checks in with this group periodically to see their progress and determine if they need additional resources or guidance.

Each group presents their work at the end of the activity, and Miss Miele and her students use a common summative assessment tool to evaluate the content, clarity, and organization of the presentations. In a differentiated classroom, the teacher customizes formative assessment, but all students are expected to perform to the same standards. The finale is a scaffolded quiz, sequenced to begin with basic vocabulary questions before progressing to more challenging questions, including a written response to an editorial.

Ensuring Fair and Respectful Learning Experiences

Providing responsive and intentional instruction is dependent on high-quality formative assessment, and so too is fairness. For Tomlinson, fairness does not mean that all students receive the same instruction but that all receive what they need—and not just at the beginning of instruction but throughout it. To do this, teachers must track individual learning and progress, a core element of assessing formatively.

Many secondary teachers I work with teach more than 100 students a day. Under these circumstances, it can be difficult to get to know all students well, and it's mostly the superstars and the sluggish learners who stand out. But sometimes a teacher may misidentify students as slower learners when, in actuality, they just don't grasp the teacher's lecture style as readily as other students do. Or perhaps they struggle to arrange their thoughts sequentially when writing an essay but would have no trouble providing the same information verbally. Bear in mind, too, that students often become very adept at disguising their deficiencies through learned strategies such as copying others' work or acting like they understand. Regular formative assessment is a means to uncover what's really going on within these students; to gain insight into their learning styles, abilities, strengths, and weaknesses; and to guide appropriate instructional responses.

There are many strategies available for differentiating both instruction and assessment, but all of them work best when a teacher has used formative assessment strategies to identify the specific differentiation that will best meet a learner's needs. In this bidirectional relationship, feedback from the formative assessment guides decisions related to content, instructional strategy, depth of instruction, and pacing.

At the Crossroads

We have taken our helicopter view and gotten a big picture of some current theories and models. We've seen that formative assessment is a point where several of these intersect. But there are many competing routes to educational improvement. Constituents are clamoring for change in education. Demands include more charter schools, more school choice, better teacher training, increased funding, national standards, critical thinking, global skills, technology, learning communities. How do we decide which initiative, theory, or reform to pursue?

Again, I offer advice from my doctoral professor: *funnel*. Take a big view of all the policy and theory and reforms, which might include No Child Left Behind (NCLB) requirements, your professional learning community (PLC) objectives or professional development goals, differentiated instruction (DI), application of multiple intelligences (MI) theory, and Response to Intervention (RTI) or Scientific Research Based Interventions (SRBI). Then funnel these through your current circumstances—that is, what's going on in your school, in your classroom—and ask yourself what needs improving (see Figure 6.4). In this way, you run content through the narrower fit of context. The goal is to arrive at the best way to improve learning for all of your students. I have no doubt that that vision will include formative assessment.

FIGURE 6.4	The Funnel of Educational Improvement

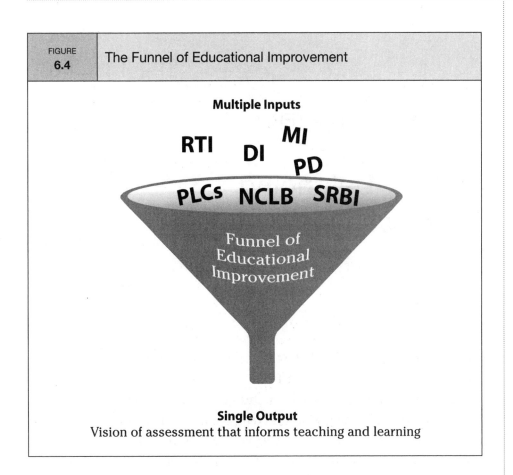

CHAPTER 7

Balancing Assessment Practices

▌▌▌

A car mechanic will tell you that a tire is out of balance when its center of rotation is different from its center of gravity. Over time, this imbalance worsens and affects other components of the car, causing wear and tear, damage, and even breakdowns. The mechanic can offer you two ways to balance the tires. In a "static balance," he simply places the tire on a fulcrum point and adjusts for disequilibrium. In a "dynamic balance," he tests the wheel under simulated road conditions. Most experts recommend the dynamic balancing system, which gives you a better sense of your car's true performance.

Traditional summative assessment offers only a static balance for our education system. At a single point in time, a student is tested and then compared to a larger group of students, generally in relation to their achievement of specific learning outcomes. Sometimes these tests claim to simulate actual conditions—authentic assessments, asking students to apply learning—but they usually ask students to demonstrate mastery by responding to only a select set of targets under artificial conditions and with unrealistic time constraints. In contrast, a dynamic, formative approach to assessment builds upon, informs, and connects to classroom instruction. It measures learning using comprehensive and continuous strategies, and it incorporates a variety of methods for measuring and reporting.

Formative assessment is gaining ground with educators as its ability to have a significant, positive effect on student learning in the classroom is becoming clearer. However, it is rarely, as yet, linked to high-stakes assessments or part of official policy at the state, district, or even school level. I believe that it is not just necessary but imperative to the health of our education system that we join these separate forms and uses of assessment into a comprehensive, dynamic, and balanced system—one focused on improving student learning.

Making Policy

As a plan or a course of action, policy is designed to guide decisions and procedures. In general, policy is fluid—modified over time as knowledge, settings, and constituents change. Because the research supporting education theories is more qualitative than quantitative, these theories are always subject to challenge, and consensus about how to interpret and apply them changes over time.

The first standardized tests, designed to measure "intelligence," appeared in the early 1900s and were used to classify students. Routine use of intelligence tests was abandoned in the 1960s in favor of a variety of other measures determined by state and local decision makers. These tests were based on minimum competencies. The early 1990s saw a resurgence of John Dewey's ideas about progressive education. His belief that education should be integrated with life, meaningful, relevant, and child focused provided a backdrop for project-based learning and authentic assessment. The original Elementary and Secondary Education Act (ESEA) of 1965 was designed to help economically disadvantaged children. Its 2001 reauthorization, known as No Child Left Behind (NCLB), has led schools toward high-stakes, mandatory standardized testing. In turn, reaction to that legislation has inspired an exploration of balanced assessment systems—ones that incorporate both school-based and standardized measurement.

Few would deny that NCLB is a powerful motivator for schools to pre-pare students for standardized testing or that the compelling sanctions are effective in driving schools toward focused instruction. However, what can be argued and documented is that these test-based accountability programs effectively narrow the curriculum (even while expanding the number of content standards teachers are expected to cover) and reduce the time teachers have to focus on the real-life applications of learning. Some educators view the recent emergence of formative assessment as an effective strategy to counterbalance the prevailing emphasis on standard-ized testing. Others believe formative assessment will contribute to improved standardized scores. Many see it as a relevant source of useful data on which to build educational decisions and thus a valuable part of a balanced assessment system. As the following sampling of assessment policy recommendations illustrates, a number of national education groups have affirmed the value of formative assessment in their recom-mendations for assessment policy:

• The Joint Committee on Standards for Educational Evaluation (2002) states, "Evaluations of students should provide information that identifies both strengths and weaknesses, so that strengths can be built upon and problem areas addressed" (p. 1).

• The National Council on Measurement in Education (1995) asserts, "Teachers [should] understand how valid assessment data can support instructional activities such as providing appropriate feedback to stu-dents, diagnosing group and individual learning needs, planning for indi-vidualized educational programs, motivating students and evaluating instructional procedures" (p. 2).

• The National Research Council's Committee on Assessment in Sup-port of Instruction and Learning, in the book *Assessment in Support of Instruction and Learning* (2003), expanded its emphasis on standardized testing to note that educators should use classroom assessment proce-dures to measure students' progress in attaining content standards not assessed by state tests.

• The National Forum on Assessment (1995) developed principles based on the premise that "the primary purpose of assessment is to improve student learning and provide information for school improvement . . . and be based on multiple methods to assess progress and use multiple ways for students to express knowledge and understanding" (p. 1).

• The Council of Chief State School Officers (2008) convened an advisory group and a collaborative working group called SCASS (State Collaborative on Assessment and Student Standards) to provide leadership and clarity on the significance and practice of formative assessment. A subgroup of SCASS, known as the FAST group (Formative Assessment for Students and Teachers), came to the conclusion that formative assessment must be regarded as a process rather than a product that "involves both teachers and students in a systematic process to improve learning" (p. 3).

Despite this widespread support for formative assessment, there are many complications to unravel before we will see a new, comprehensive formative assessment policy written and implemented at a national level. What I recommend is that while educators await this new policy, we start making changes to our own practice now. In lieu of a castigatory national model, it is time for schools, districts, and states to build assessment models that are informative, improve learning, and incorporate a variety of strategies. Rather than reacting to external mandates, we must internalize student learning needs and act in ways that strengthen our ability to meet those needs.

REMEMBER

In thinking about formative assessment policy, ask

- Is it focused on the classroom teacher and student?
- Is it based on curriculum standards that are realistic and attainable?
- Is it fully aligned and articulated across all curriculum standards?
- Does it identify learning gaps and guide strategies for closing them?
- Does it engage students in the assessment process?
- Are the associated assessments valid, reliable, fair, and feasible?
- Is it driven by research-based strategies that are flexible and portable across grade levels and content areas?

From "Reporting Out" to "Reporting In"

For the most part, assessment in education has been a "reporting out" process. Teachers tell students the grades they've earned, parents receive students' report cards, and administrators report standardized test scores to the community and state. An alternative is the "reporting in" process of formative assessment, in which data are maintained in house and used to adjust instruction and improve learning. With ready access to data, teachers and other school leaders can review it regularly, looking for evidence of learning growth and gaps. Their findings can inform decisions related to everything from the next day's lesson or applied activity to long-range planning to annual teacher goals.

Most secondary schools rely on standardized test results and report cards for data about student learning, but these sources have limitations. Standardized test data give a numerical snapshot of a student's achievement and can be useful to teachers and students, especially when dissected into standards and reported by competency. However, secondary students may be given a standardized test only once during their enrollment. Teachers usually prepare report cards four times a year, but these reports typically have a letter or numerical grade along with one or two comments that are electronically selected. Compared to elementary school report cards, which often have narratives on students' progress toward specific standards—in part based on numerous measures like DIBELS (Dynamic Indicators of Basic Early Literacy Skills) and DRPs (Degrees of Reading Power), secondary-level report cards give little concrete information. Educators in middle and high schools need more than these two sources provide. They—especially—need to gather and report in more data.

Dealing with Data

It's easy to say, "Collect more data," but I know this task is often overwhelming. Even for teachers who feel confident about incorporating formative assessment in their classrooms, compiling and tracking data on learning can be daunting. Recently I presented a workshop on formative assessment to a group of teachers and toward the end, assigned an applied activity that offered them a choice between two options:

Option 1: Write a lesson plan that incorporates formative assessment before, during, and after instruction.

Option 2: Identify ways to change what and how you are teaching in response to data gathered from the following sources: standardized tests, school and grade testing, common assessments, classroom summative assessments, classroom formative assessments, teacher observations, authentic assessment, homework, and prior information about a student.

There were 12 working groups of teachers participating in this workshop, and all 12 groups picked Option 1, writing a lesson plan.

Reluctance to deal with data is understandable, but in a balanced assessment system—one in which decisions at all levels are informed by results from many measures of learning, both formative and summative—it's imperative that we be able to organize and analyze the data we collect. If you think of data in terms of what you would like to know, the task of data interpretation becomes more manageable, and the resulting charts and tables and matrixes are very useful.

Before collecting data, you need to be clear about your purpose. It may be to track learning or to identify gaps in learning. It may be to follow selected students over time or to determine what strategies are most effective. Whatever your purpose, it should be specific to a goal or a student. Data must be collected and analyzed in a timely manner and must be used to inform a concrete response.

REMEMBER

Before you gather data, ask yourself

- What do I want to measure? What standards, goals, or objectives?
- What is my purpose in collecting information?
- What data do I need?
- How and where will I get the data? What sources will I use?
- How will I respond to the data?

Once you have identified a clear purpose for gathering and using data, you can choose a collection strategy. Data collection and analysis ought to reflect the purpose and desired outcomes. You might track the progress of each class, based on a variety of measures including standardized scores, prior grades, schoolwide expectations, classroom tests, projects, presentations, and social skills. As your need for information changes, so too will the way you organize it.

To get you started, let's look at how data management can provide teachers with formative data on student needs and progress. In her 6th grade math class, Ms. Nacatta uses several strategies to gather and chart progress. Early in the year, she gives a pre-assessment focused on the key skills of the 5th grade math curriculum. First she organizes the resulting data in a chart to show whole-class achievement (see Figure 7.1). There, she records the number of children who gave correct answers to problems requiring a specific skill, like double-digit multiplication, and also makes notes about common errors.

The completed chart shows her whole-class gaps in learning in specific skills. Ms. Nacatta begins each class session that week with a warm-up

FIGURE 7.1	Analysis of Whole-Class Pre-assessment Data

Ms. Nacatta's 6th grade math class: Skill Quiz
Week 1: Review of prior knowledge

Type of problem	# Answering Correctly (out of 20 students)	Comments
Subtracting fractions	10	2 had no simplest form
Probability	8	reading difficulties
Double-digit multiplication	16	3 had regrouping errors
Subtracting decimals	10	computational errors
Estimating products	12	
Place value	3	
Equivalent fractions	10	
Percent to decimal	15	5 had no zero

focused on those areas. The first skill on her list is place value. Because the pre-assessment also pointed out that students are struggling with simple computation, as she introduces the idea of place value, she uses a strategy that she calls Mad Minute to measure their calculation speed and accuracy in response to targeted questions. Students chart their Mad Minute times, and increases in speed and accuracy are cause for classwide celebration.

Based on these Mad Minute assessment records, Ms. Nacatta recognizes that although all students are making progress, some still have big hurdles to overcome. She begins to track students' individual progress on standards using a chart (see the excerpt in Figure 7.2). She codes the table cells, using different kinds of shading to indicate higher scores and lower scores. This makes patterns of strengths and weaknesses evident and helps her identify students with similar skill levels.

FIGURE 7.2	Matrix of Individual Student Progress Toward Standards				

Ms. Nacatta's 6th grade math class: Skill Quiz
Week 2: Baseline measures

Name	Standard: Subtracting fractions	Standard: Probability	Standard: Double-digit multiplication	Standard: Estimation	Standard: Place value
Wilson	4	5	6	10	3
Latham	7	7	4	5	4
Paris	8	4	5	9	3
Bennett	3	6	7	7	2
Brooklyn	6	6	7	5	1
Sundance	5	8	7	6	4
Madison	7	7	5	8	5
Berkeley	8	4	6	9	5
+Students . . .					

Student's highest-scoring standard

Student's lowest-scoring standard

Ms. Nacatta then decides to set up an interventions planning sheet to track how she will address each student's needs and how effective the intervention is. She creates a table and enters the standard, the student name, the probable cause of difficulty, the instructional response or intervention she will use (e.g., small-group review, tutoring), and how she will measure the effectiveness of the response (see Figure 7.3). This table gives Ms. Nacatta a record of her instructional responses that she can use to reconsider the cause of a student's gap or the intervention employed to address it.

Having information about the success of her instructional responses leads Ms. Nacatta to wonder what learning progress will look like over time for each student and for each standard. She creates a matrix of teaching and learning outcomes for particular standards (see the excerpt in Figure 7.4), and there, she records relative scores on the course pre-assessment and results from the various formative assessment measures used during instruction aimed at each standard. She also tracks the instructional adjustments she makes in response to the formative assessment

FIGURE 7.3	Planned Instructional Interventions			
Ms. Nacatta's 6th grade math class Weeks 2–3: Interventions planning sheet				
Areas for Intervention	**Student or Group**	**Reflection/Cause**	**Intervention Strategies**	**Measure of Intervention Effectiveness**
Compound interest		Difficulty with exponents	Small-group review of exponents	Achievement on review sheet
Subtracting fractions	Bennett	Simplifying fractions	Put out pie puzzle game	Recording of game results
Place value	Bennett Brooklyn Wilson Paris	Number sets	Small-group review with hands-on activity	Retest
Probability	Paris Berkeley	Peer support team-up with Sundance	Dice and coin toss activity	Recording of activity data; two additional application problems

FIGURE 7.4	Matrix of Student Outcomes by Standard								

Ms. Nacatta's 6th grade math class
Results of assessments and interventions for individual students by standard

Student	Std#	PA	FA	INT	Sum	Std#	PA	FA	INT	Sum
Latham	1.2	6	7	P	8	1.3				
Madison	1.2	3	6	T	7	1.3				
Berkeley	1.2	8	9	E	10	1.3				
Wilson	1.2	10	10	E	10	1.3				
Bennett	1.2	5	6	PO	8	1.3				

Table abbreviations:
Std = standard/benchmark/goal
Results (1–10 scale): PA = pre-assessment result; FA = formative assessment (during/after instruction) result; Sum = summative assessment result; INT = instructional intervention: P = peer; T = tutoring; E = enrichment; PO = pull-out

data to help her determine how effective her interventions are. The measure of effectiveness, she decides, will be scores on the standard's final, summative test.

At the end of this process, the completed matrix gives her a lot of information about student progress over the entire unit of instruction. She decides to share with each student his or her own progress. This is especially important to Madison, who has improved her skills the most; seeing the data helps her gain even more confidence. Ms. Nacatta decides to factor growth in learning into her final grades and to have students chart their own progress next year.

Finally, Ms. Nacatta wants to see how the results of various assessments of students' learning for each standard align. She sets up spreadsheets where she can record data from multiple sources, including formative and summative assessment, grades, and state standardized test results. Using these spreadsheets, she generates custom reports, capable of displaying the data by subgroup, data type (classroom-generated or standardized), report card information, and so on. All this information lets her see how classroom assessments align with common assessments at the school level and state standardized tests. It also shows her where any groupwide gaps are so that she can plan an appropriate instructional response.

When Ms. Nacatta shares her data with the math team at her school, the team decides all teachers should track learning progress by specific standards for individual students. This record will give teachers an excellent source of information about individual student strengths and weaknesses and student response to specific strategies. They decide to maintain these data over the students' enrollment so teachers at different grade levels can refer to them. The data will also give the team a foundation for evaluating and adjusting curriculum and practice across grade levels.

In short, Ms. Nacatta's efforts to use data to inform her instruction result in records of learning that are highly informative at the classroom, school, and even district level:

• At the classroom level, the tables, charts and matrixes show areas for instructional intervention, change, and differentiation.

• At the schoolwide level, a comparison of teachers' records can guide changes in curriculum, textbook selection, goals, and strategies.

• At the district level, data from many teachers and schools can inform professional development.

These records are also beneficial to students and their families. Being able to pinpoint a student's strengths and knowledge gaps, to see which learning strategies and assessments work best for a student, and most of all, to have evidence of a student's progress can all help to inform parents' and students' decisions about how to maximize learning.

Informing Curricular Review

Educators have many tools for designing, aligning, and articulating curriculum. Sequencing, learning progressions, scope, and maps are a few of them. Each is intended to guide teachers toward appropriate content in a logical and consistent order. Generally based on standards, these tools focus on the big ideas, ways to build learning and make and measure progress across grade levels. They take a schoolwide or districtwide view of instruction, assessment, and learning.

Although curricula are usually designed with care, schools and districts seldom revisit them. Rather than looking at a curriculum as a completed product, educators should view it as a living document to be continually reviewed and adjusted in response to data. Information about student achievement toward benchmarks and standards should be reported in from teachers and schools to inform ongoing decisions about a curriculum's effectiveness and implementation.

Heidi Hayes Jacobs (2004) endorses a mapping format for curriculum planning that includes the subject, unit, standards, content, learning activities, and assessments. She points out, "What is often missing in assessment and testing is a formal interim level of work at the school level. Because mapping provides the opportunity for a specific school to closely examine its students, it is possible to generate site-specific diagnosis and prescriptions" (p. 113). If formative and summative data from teachers show that students are struggling with a particular standard—say, word problems—then instructional changes and adjustments must occur. Perhaps more time should be planned for teaching the standard, or perhaps the curriculum should be adjusted to ensure the foundation for these skills is provided earlier in the school year. If the data indicate large numbers of learning gaps, it may mean that the curriculum maps need to be adjusted.

One issue that might become apparent in reviewing reported-in data is the sheer number of standards covered. Focusing on depth or big-picture standards may be a better approach than having so many individual standards in divergent content areas. For instance, in social studies, rather than focusing on presidents, national budgets, foreign relations, and individual rights, the big-picture standard could be to analyze how governments affect and reflect the political and economic values of a country. With a clearer idea of what data are important to collect and analyze, teachers and school leaders can gather these data more consistently, target particular standards and students, and design more effective interventions.

Whatever the determined cause of a gap between learning and expectations of learning, when reported-in data indicate a gulf, an immediate response is possible. Rather than waiting for district and state reports, schools can have timely and ongoing feedback and make a timely response.

When formative assessment results combined with other data sources in a balanced system indicate learning is not progressing, educators have many options for responding. They can

- Change classroom instruction and assessment
- Alter grade-level expectations and change resources
- Change curriculum and adjust sequence
- Adjust curriculum maps

Another advantage of reporting in data from multiple sources is that teachers, principals, and district office staff are all using the same information in the same way to improve learning through responsive action. A study by Englert, Fries, Martin-Glenn, and Michael (2005) points out that each of the three levels in an educational system typically use data in different ways. Superintendents use data to allocate resources, select curricula, and evaluate personnel. Principals are more apt to use data to help them understand their teachers' instructional practices and how accountability principles are actualizing in their school. And teachers generally use data the least, primarily to gather information about their students. All educators in the same system need to have and use the most complete picture of student learning they can assemble, and all should use it to inform decisions. Formative assessment data are a key part of the information a balanced system of assessment should yield.

Training Teachers

In carrying out a balanced assessment system, schools and districts will need teachers who are trained to assess formatively and to effectively use formative data from multiple sources to inform their instruction. Like education policy, teacher training also has had swings in emphasis. As teacher colleges of the 1950s and '60s have developed into today's undergraduate and graduate schools of education, the focus of these programs has evolved from teaching basic reading, writing, and arithmetic to applied learning. And recently, NCLB has redirected teacher training to a concentration on basic literacy and numeracy. Today's programs also focus less on pedagogy and more on subject-specific content. Most states now require Praxis (or similar) content area testing of their teachers, and many states require that their teachers major in a content area prior to beginning their studies in education. Amid these changes, little attention has been given to teaching teachers to assess.

Research on classroom assessment illustrates the lack of teacher training in this area. Most teachers use traditional tests with selected-choice questions and lack the knowledge and skill to assess effectively (Guskey, 2003; McMillan & Workman, 1998; Stiggins, 2001). The imperative to improve preservice training is clear. I was recently working with a new teacher on her portfolio of teaching and learning. She was struggling with the assessment piece and bemoaning the fact that her teacher-preparation classes included a lot of discussion of teaching in the content area but little emphasis on how this applied to assessment practice on a daily basis.

Inservice professional development also needs improving. Teachers identify inservice training on assessment as a weak link in their ongoing development of knowledge and improvement of practice. They also report that most of what they know about assessment they learned from other teachers (Greenstein, 2005). Schools need to provide professional development in all areas of assessment, including valid assessment, standards-based assessment, alternative strategies, rubrics, grading practices, feedback, and motivation. All are essential components of a balanced assessment system.

Most importantly, teacher training can't consist solely of a one-time professional development session. Teachers need continued support and follow-up afterward. Indeed, teacher learning and progress should be tracked and scaffolded, just as students' learning should be. Customized and individualized professional development, as well as professional learning communities (PLCs), can be effective ways to develop essential teacher knowledge of formative assessment. Ultimately, formative assessment needs to be built into the training process. We need to make professional development student focused, provide ongoing feedback, and monitor and measure outcomes in practice in the classroom.

When training teachers in formative assessment

- Stress that teaching and learning are interconnected
- Set expectations for classroom practice
- Provide exemplars, role models, and mentors at all levels
- Encourage teacher collaboration through PLCs
- Institute supportive values, beliefs, actions, and structures
- Assess results in a balanced and transparent manner

Why Change?

There is much work to do to make our assessment system a balanced one. We must train teachers in gathering data before, during, and after instruction and in using those data to inform decisions about teaching. We must use classroom data as evidence in making curricular changes and changes in instruction. We must continue to research formative assessment's effectiveness and identify best practices in using it. But most importantly, we must remember that formative assessment and a balanced system are about improving each student's learning.

In closing, I would like to revisit Mei and Ernesto, the two 8th grade math students we met in the Introduction. They have spent half a year in Mr. Major's formative classroom. As Mr. Major has consistently implemented formative assessment using different strategies, given feedback, and adjusted and customized instruction and assessments, there has been documented growth in Mei's and Ernesto's learning and skills. And they have experienced another change—an increase in motivation and self-efficacy. When asked to reflect on their progress and attitude toward math, they gave the following responses:

Mei: I've been taught to be respectful of teachers, but in this class I really felt that the teacher was respectful of me and my needs. I liked the way we started with a review, and it was fun to play games during class, like Bump in the Road. I got to know more people in this class because we worked with different groups.

Sometimes I felt like I was the smart one in the group and helped others with a particular problem. Other times, I sat back and listened and learned from others. I feel better about math than I have in a long time.

Ernesto: Well, I guess I'm not as stupid as I thought. I knew I was smart in some ways. I could talk people into doing things my way, but sometimes that got me into trouble. I know that math isn't for me, but I know that there are some things I can do really well. I like this class because the teacher was very flexible in how I could learn. Sometimes he had me work with others, and sometimes he let me puzzle it out for myself, but help was always available. I felt proud when he told me what I was good at. Instead of just grading a test with a bad grade, he told me what I could do to do better. I could still clown around a little, but I didn't do it so much in this class as in my other classes. I don't know why.

Throughout this book, I have described the kinds of changes we need in assessment practices. Taking the steps to make change happen is the challenge facing teachers and educational leaders. Roland Barth (2002) said that "probably the most important and the most difficult job of an instructional leader is to change the prevailing culture of a school" (p. 6). He continued on to explain what is required for cultural change: high-quality curriculum, high-quality assessment information about student learning, and teachers working together to innovate and improve teaching practices. When change in our assessment practice and policy can effect such meaningful change for our students, how can we not take up this challenge?

Appendix A

Glossary of Assessment Terms

Having a common "language of assessment," consistently used and understood, facilitates meaningful and accurate communication. The following definitions are derived from my own work, conventional wisdom, and numerous references in books and online.

alternative assessment: Assessment other than traditional pencil-and-paper tests. This includes a wide array of activities such as projects, portfolios, posters, presentations, and journals.

assessment: The measurement of the outcomes of teaching and learning. Activities of teachers, students, districts, and states that involve gathering and analyzing information about student performance that is useful regarding the improvement of teaching and learning.

assessment systems: "The combination of multiple assessments into a comprehensive reporting format that produces comprehensive, dependable information upon which important decisions can be made about students, schools, districts, or states" (National

Center for Research on Evaluation Standards, and Student Testing, 2001, p. 1).

authentic assessment: Demonstration of mastery of a real-world task. Authentic assessment replicates the challenges and standards of problem-solving skills and competencies in a context that individuals could face in everyday circumstances.

classroom assessment: Assessments developed, administered, and scored by teachers for the purpose of evaluating individual or classroom performance on a topic.

common assessments: Assessments collaboratively developed by teachers teaching the same subject and grade that are given collectively to students to assess progress toward standards. They can be used in a formative or summative manner.

content validity: Content-related validity "refers to the extent to which the test questions represent the skills in the specified subject area" (Rudner & Schafer, 2002, p. 12). Essentially, the question of content validity asks whether the test is measuring what it is supposed to measure.

criterion-referenced test: An assessment that compares "an individual's performance . . . to a specific learning objective, performance standard, or established criteria" (National Center for Research on Evaluation, Standards, and Student Testing, 2001, p. 1). Criterion-referenced tests determine how well a student does "relative to a predetermined performance level on a specified set of educational goals or outcomes included in the school, district, or state curriculum" (Rudner & Schafer, 2002, p. 21).

differentiated instruction: A teacher's response to the needs of diverse learners with the goal of maximizing student growth and individual success. Differentiated instruction is guided by the general principles of respectful tasks, flexible grouping, ongoing assessment, and adjustment.

exhibitions: Student-created displays and products that demonstrate their competencies.

formative assessment: A systematic and planned process used by teachers and students to gather evidence of learning, engage students in assessment, and improve teaching and learning based on data collected.

performances: Students perform meaningful tasks that incorporate skills and knowledge to demonstrate mastery of pre-established standards. Performances include public exhibitions of student work.

portfolios: A selective collection of an individual student's work over a specific period of time. Portfolios can include a variety of work (e.g., written, audio, or video material) and can be collected by the teacher or collaboratively. Teachers can use portfolios as an assessment technique to measure student progress over time.

projects: Complex pieces of work that students complete alone or in a group. Projects demonstrate and apply prior and recent learning.

reliability: A measure of consistency. "Reliability is the extent to which the measurements resulting from a test are the result of characteristics of those being measured." It is also defined as "the degree to which test scores for a group of test takers are consistent over repeated applications of a measurement procedure" (Rudner & Shafer, 2002, p. 16).

selected-response items: Test questions that contain the correct answer as part of the question. Examples include true/false, multiple-choice, and matching items.

standardized test: A form of measurement that has been normed against a particular population or criteria. All students in a population are given the same test, and equivalent scores are produced to allow comparison between students or groups. Standardized means that the test uses "uniform procedures for administration and scoring in order to assure that the results from different people are comparable" (Rudner & Schafer, 2002, p. 21).

summative assessment: The collection of evidence of learning after a period of instruction. It is generally used to judge learning outcomes and determine a score.

validity: "Test validity refers to the degree to which the inferences based on test scores are meaningful, useful, and appropriate. Thus, test validity is a characteristic of a test when it is administered to a particular population" (Rudner & Shafer, 2002, p. 12).

Appendix B
Lexicon of Formative Assessment Strategies

The strategies outlined here represent a compilation of readily available ideas combined with some of my original ones. The book *Differentiated Assessment Strategies* (Chapman & King, 2005) and the Glossary of Instructional Strategies, maintained by PlasmaLink Web Services (2007), were particularly helpful in the assembly of this lexicon. Please note that strategies listed here are flexible. Adapt them to fit your assessment needs and your students.

3-2-1

Students write three key terms related to what they know or have learned, two questions they have, and one way they can apply their learning. Variations include asking for three facts, two concepts, and one question.

10 + 2

The teacher presents information for 10 minutes and then asks students to summarize, reflect on, or apply the information for two minutes. Teachers can vary timing and content to meet instructional goals. Common variations include 20 + 5 and 5 + 1.

A-B-C Summary

Students think of a word related to the topic of study for each letter of the alphabet. Students can also think of a lesson-related word for each letter of a unit vocabulary word.

Acronym/Abbreviation Summaries

Students create an acronym or abbreviation to summarize the main points of a topic. For example, a health class studying nutrients devised the acronym *B-Train* to sum up what they learned about B vitamins. *B-Train* comes from B-TRN, which stands for B (vitamins) = T(hiamin), R(iboflavin), and N(iacin). This technique is also a good memorization tool.

Application Cards

Students think of one way to apply their new knowledge or skill in the real world and write it down on an index card. The teacher collects the cards and either shares them anonymously with the class or keeps them to review privately.

Ball Toss

To start the activity, the teacher gives the ball to a student and asks a question. The student can answer the question and toss the ball to a student of his choice, who will answer the next question, or he can decide not to answer the question and toss it. The teacher allows the students only a set number of passes on questions. Teacher- or student-generated questions can be used.

Bump in the Road

Students write down something from the lesson that they find confusing or a skill or concept that they find difficult. Teachers can collect the responses to review, or they can form small groups and ask students to share their "bumps" and seek clarification. If everyone in a group has the same problem, then the group shares it with the whole class.

Categories

Students are challenged to come up with a word or term that corresponds to categories aligned with key content. Teachers may generate these categories, setting them up in a grid:

Ecosystem	Climate	Animal	Edible
Wetlands			
Desert			
Grassland			

As students become familiar with the strategy, they can come up with some or all categories and set up grids on their own. Grids can be completed individually or in small groups. In a variation of this strategy that recalls the board game Scattergories, teachers provide only a letter for some or all of the grid categories, and students respond with content-related words, terms, or phrases that begin with that letter:

Ecosystem	E	C	O
Wetlands			
Desert			
Grassland			

Chunking/Clustering (*see also* Graphic organizers)

A technique where students are asked to group information graphically into chunks or clusters, sorting it by categories or attributes. This helps to clarify connections and relationships and supports memorization.

Color-Coding

Students use color tags to label objects or ideas that belong together.

Concentration

The teacher makes pairs of cards with the name of a concept on one and the description of the concept on the other. Students place cards facedown on a table and take turns choosing two cards to flip over. If the cards match and the student correctly identifies them as matching, the student keeps the cards. If the cards do not match, the student puts the cards facedown again.

Continuum

Students arrange cards with key words to form a continuum based on selected criteria. For example, *apple, peach, grape,* and *cantaloupe* can be arranged by size, color, or growing conditions (temperate to tropical).

Cooperative Review (*see also* Q&A Mix-Up)

Student groups write questions and take turns asking other groups their questions. This strategy can be conducted as a game, with points awarded, or as a review for a test.

Corners

The teacher labels various corners of the classroom with "Disagree," "Agree," and "Unsure" (or other relevant labels) and then reads a statement and asks students to go to the corner that best represents their response. All students sharing a similar point of view work together to collect evidence and present an argument supporting their beliefs.

Critiques

Students analyze, interpret, or evaluate the work of experts, peers, or self. Critiques can be formal or informal, written or oral, but are most effective when based on a common rubric and when feedback is descriptive of process and product.

Empty Outlines

The teacher gives students a partially completed outline of a lesson, and students fill in the missing content as it's presented. This strategy can be combined with a Think–Pair–Share after the lesson to compare answers or problem spots.

Entrance Slips/Exit Slips

Students write a response to a teacher-generated question on a slip of paper. The teacher can review answers privately or share some with the whole class anonymously to start a discussion. Entrance slip questions relate to upcoming learning. Exit slip questions relate to completed instruction. In a variation, teachers can use the same question as both an entrance and exit slip to measure growth in learning.

Feathers and Salt

Students reflect on and identify two concepts or skills that they are soaring with, feeling confident of their understanding (feathers). They also identify one concept or skill that is pulling them down (the salt on their tail). Students can share privately with the teacher, or the teacher can share responses anonymously with the class.

Fingers-Up

Students indicate their degree of understanding on a scale of zero to five by holding up the corresponding number of fingers. Student can close their eyes for anonymity.

Gallery/Graffiti Wall

Students make a display of their knowledge or beliefs. They can create these individually or make a common display, or graffiti wall.

Games

Students create games such as *Jeopardy* and Trivial Pursuit to demonstrate understanding. Completed games can be used as a review.

Grab Bag

In this review activity, students reach into a paper bag and draw a piece of paper on which they or the teacher have written a lesson-related question, answer, name, fact, concept, or any combination of these. Each student responds to the slip he or she has drawn by answering the question, providing a question for an answer, finding a classmate who has drawn the answer to his or her question (see Q&A Mix-Up), or explaining the significance of the lesson-related information. In a variation, teachers select objects that relate to lesson content and put them in a bag. Students take turns drawing an object from the bag and explaining or illustrating how the object relates to what they have learned.

Graphic organizers

Students create graphic organizers of their knowledge and understanding. These reveal connections and relationships between concepts and can take many formats: Venn diagrams, webs, concept maps, clusters or chunks, bubbles, trees, brackets, tables, flow charts, timelines, T charts, spiders, sequences, continuums, cycles, and so on.

Grouping/Sequencing

Students use new learning to group information in various ways, depending on directions provided. Grouping possibilities include chronological order, sequential order, general to specific, part to whole, spiral, step by step, and so on.

Idea Spinner

The teacher makes a spinner divided into four quadrants with labels such as "Vocabulary," "Main Idea," "Application," "Interdisciplinary Connection" or "Calculate," "Summarize," "Apply," or "Evaluate." Students spin to see what type or category of questions they will be asked. The teacher can differentiate the level of task difficulty.

Inside-Outside Circle

Each student writes a review question with the correct answer on a card. (The teacher needs to check cards for accuracy.) Students form two concentric circles, about equal in size, with students in the inner circle facing students in the outer circle. Students facing one another pair up ask each other their questions. The outside circle moves to create new pairs until everyone has been asked all the questions.

Inverted Pyramid

Students write down what they know, starting with the most important information, followed by the next most important, and closing with the least important information.

Journaling

Students write their thoughts about their learning in a designated notebook or journal. Specific prompts can help students focus their thoughts. Students share journal entries with the teacher, and the teacher provides feedback.

Jumbled Summary

Teachers present random words from instruction (either verbally or in writing). Students put these key words and phrases into a logical sequence.

K-W-L

Students identify what they know (K), what they want to know (W), and what learning activity they will use to find out (L). Students can work individually and pass in responses to the teacher or work in small groups and then share responses or post them collectively and walkabout to view them. Variations include K-W-H-L and K-W-H-L-S, or know, want to know, how to find out, learned, and still want to learn.

Layman's Translation/Martian News

Students write a simplified summary of what they have learned or explain what they have just learned to a Martian just arrived on Earth who has no previous knowledge of the topic.

Line-Up

The teacher gives student teams cards with sequential ideas that can be put in order. Each student receives a card, and then the team lines up to put the concepts in order. With multiple teams, sequences can be compared and discussed.

Memory Matrix

Five to eight students volunteer to summarize the main ideas of instruction and share something they learned. A new group of volunteers (the same number) restate what the first volunteers summarized and shared.

Minute Papers

At the end of class, students write for one minute in response to prompts such as "What did you learn today? "What is most/least useful?" or "Why is this important?"

Muddiest Point

Students name or describe the concept they have the least understanding of, or their muddiest point. Students can share their muddiest points with the class, or the teacher can collect them and review them privately.

Multiple Response Cards

The teacher prepares sets of cards with short answers to questions (several cards can have the same answer) and passes several out to each student. During the lesson, the teacher asks questions, and students review their cards to see if they have the answer. If they do, they hold up the card. Cards can also be color-coded so that when the answers are held up, the teacher can scan colors quickly for correct answers.

Nutshelling

Students write or orally give a summary of their learning that captures the main point or essence of the material.

One Word

Students write one word that summarizes their learning and then explain why they chose that word.

Paraphrasing

Students restate important information in their own words.

Post-Test Review

On completing a test or quiz, students identify the most difficult or challenging question by marking it with an asterisk on their paper. The teacher gathers the tests and, for the questions with the most asterisks, gives prompts, reminders, or examples (but not answers) to review. Tests are returned to students so that they may change their responses before handing in the test for grading.

Pros and Cons

Students generate lists of arguments for or against a course of action or set of assertions. They then can rank them, evaluate the short list, and screen out arguments based on information available or found in research.

Q&A Mix-Up

Students write a review question on a colored index card and the answer to it on a card of a different color. The teacher checks answers for accuracy and then collects only the answers and redistributes them. To start, one volunteer reads her question. All students look at their answer cards, and whoever thinks he has the answer raises his card and is called on. If the student is correct, he asks his question and the round continues. The teacher can review any questions that students are unable to match.

Questioning Baseball

The teacher asks a question of one student at a time; students may hit at it (guess with no penalty), pass it on to the designated hitter or next player (this happens one time), or hit it out to the crowd (all participants) to find someone who can catch it and answer the question. Teachers can differentiate the questions. It's fun to play with a foam ball.

Quickdraw/Quicktalk/Quickwrite

In pairs or small groups, students have a short period of time—two to three minutes—to share all they know about a topic using drawings or symbols (Quickdraw), spoken words (Quicktalk), or written words and graphic organizers (Quickwrite).

Recall, Summarize, Question, Connect, and Comment (RSQCC)

At the end of instruction, students *recall* (list) key points, *summarize* each point in a single sentence, ask unanswered *questions, connect* the material to the learning objectives, and write a concluding *comment.*

Scripted Cooperative Dyads

In pairs, students read assigned material. They then alternate taking the role of speaker (who summarizes and explains what was read) and listener (who listens and then corrects or adds to what the speaker said).

Share–Pair Circles

The teacher divides the class into two equal groups, and each group forms a circle. The inner circle faces outward and the outer circle faces inward to form pairs of facing students. In response to teacher prompts (which could be a concept, a question, or a controversy), each pair discusses their ideas, and then one of the circles rotates to create new pairs. Repeat until the original pairs are again facing each other.

Stars and Wishes

Students identify two things they especially liked about another student's work or two significant things they learned from it. They then make one wish for improvement (e.g., requesting more of a successful part or clarification of a confusing point).

Stir the Teams

The teacher forms groups of four students. Each student on a team has a number. Teams work together to prepare a summary of a reading or of learning or an answer to a teacher question. When the teams have completed their assignment, the teacher calls a number and the student with that number rotates to the next group. The procedure then repeats.

Think–Pair–Share

In response to a teacher prompt or question, students think individually, then pair (discuss with a partner), and then share ideas with the whole class.

Values Continuum

The teacher asks students to place themselves on a continuum (a piece of tape across the floor of the classroom) from strongly agree to strongly disagree in response to a teacher-presented statement. Students at various points on the continuum share and support their beliefs.

Voting cards

Voting cards are tools students can use to signal degrees of understanding. Typically, teachers give each student a set of colored voting cards. During instruction, the teacher asks students to use their cards to show their response to teacher statements. When students agree with a statement, they hold up a green card. When they disagree, they hold up a red card. And if they are unsure, they hold up a yellow card.

Work-Along

Students use this tool—a teacher-prepared collection of lesson or unit objectives with corresponding assignments and activities—to monitor and track their learning on an ongoing basis.

References

Ainsworth, L., & Viegut, D. (2006). *Common formative assessments: How to connect standards-based instruction and assessment.* Thousand Oaks, CA: Corwin Press.

ASCD. (2009). *2009 ASCD legislative agenda.* Alexandria, VA: Author. Available: http://www.ascd.org/public_policy/

Bandura, A. (1994). Self-efficacy. In V. S. Ramachandran (Ed.), *Encyclopedia of human behavior, Volume 4* (pp. 71–81). New York: Academic Press.

Barth, R. S. (2002, May). The culture builder. *Educational Leadership, 59*(8), 6–11.

Black, P., Harrison, C., Lee, C., Marshall, B., & Wiliam, D. (2003, April). *A successful intervention—Why did it work?* Paper presented at the annual meeting of the American Educational Research Association, Chicago.

Black, P., Harrison, C., Lee, C., Marshall, B., & Wiliam, D. (2004, September). Working inside the black box: Assessment for learning in the classroom. *Phi Delta Kappan, 86*(1), 8–21.

Black, P., & Wiliam, D. (1998, October). Inside the black box: Raising standards through classroom assessment. *Phi Delta Kappan, 80*(2), 139–148.

Bloom, B. S. (1976). *Human characteristics and school learning.* New York: McGraw-Hill.

Bloom, B. S. (1977). Favorable learning conditions for all. *Teacher, 95*(3), 22–28.

Bloom, B. S., Englehart, M. D., Furst, E. J., Hill, W. H., & Krathwohl, D. R. (Eds.). (1956). *Taxonomy of educational objectives: The classification of educational goals. Handbook I: Cognitive domain.* New York: David McKay.

Bloom, B. S., Hastings, J. T., & Madaus, G. F. (Eds.). (1971). *Handbook on formative and summative evaluation of student learning.* New York: McGraw-Hill.

Bloom, B. S., & Krathwohl, D. R. (1956). *Taxonomy of educational objectives: The classification of educational goals. Handbook II: Affective domain.* New York: David McKay.

Boston, C. (2002). The concept of formative assessment. *Practical Assessment, Research & Evaluation, 8*(9). Available: http://pareonline.net/getvn.asp?v=8&n=9

Bransford, J. D., Brown, A. L., & Cocking, R. R. (Eds.). (1999). *How people learn.* National Research Council. Washington, DC: National Academy Press.

Brookhart, S. M. (1997). A theoretical framework for the role of classroom assessment in motivating student effort and achievement. *Applied Measurement in Education, 10*(2), 161–180.

Brookhart, S. M., & Durkin, D. T. (2003, January). Classroom assessment, student motivation, and achievement in high school social studies classes. *Applied Measurement in Education, 16*(1), 27–54.

Caine, R. N., & Caine, G. (1991). *Making connections: Teaching and the human brain.* Alexandria, VA: ASCD.

Center for Evaluation and Education Policy. (2005). *High school survey of student engagement.* Bloomington, IN: Indiana University. Available: http://ceep.indiana.edu/hssse/

Chapman, C., & King, R. (2005). *Differentiated assessment strategies.* Thousand Oaks, CA: Corwin Press.

Cooney, S., & Bottoms, G. (2003). *Making middle grades work.* Atlanta: Southern Regional Education Board.

Cotton, K. (2002). Classroom questioning. *School Improvement Series, Close-Up #5.* Portland, OR: Northwest Regional Educational Laboratory.

Council of Chief State School Officers. (2008). *Attributes of effective formative assessment.* Washington, DC: Author. Available: http://www.ccsso.org/publications/details.cfm?PublicationID=362

Covey, S. R. (1989). *The 7 habits of highly effective people: Restoring the character ethic.* New York: Simon and Schuster.

Crooks, T. J. (1988). The impact of classroom evaluation practices on students. *Review of Educational Research, 58*(4), 438–481.

Darling-Hammond, L. (2004). Standards, accountability and school reform. *The Teachers College Record, 106*(6), 1047–1085.

Dweck, C. S. (2002). Messages that motivate: How praise molds students' beliefs, motivation and performance (in surprising ways). In J. Aronson (Ed.), *Improving academic achievement: Impact of psychological factors on education* (pp. 38–58). New York: Academic Press.

Englert, K., Fries, D., Martin-Glenn, M., & Michael, S. (2005, November 17). *How are educators using data? A comparative analysis of superintendent, principal, and teachers' perceptions of accountability systems.* Aurora, CO: Midcontinent Research for Education and Learning. Available: http://www.mcrel.org/topics/assessment/products/226

Gardner, H. (1983). *Frames of mind: The theory of multiple intelligences.* New York: Basic Books.

Gardner, H. (1993). *Multiple intelligences: The theory in practice.* New York: Basic Books.

Gladwell, M. (2002). *The tipping point: How little things can make a big difference.* New York: Little Brown.

Graue, M. E. (1993). Integrating theory and practice through instructional assessment. *Educational Assessment, 1,* 293–309.

Greenstein, L. (2005). Finding balance in classroom assessment: High school teachers' knowledge and practice. Unpublished doctoral dissertation.

Guskey, T. R. (2003, February). How classroom assessments improve learning. *Educational Leadership, 60*(5), 6–11.

Heritage, M. (2007). Formative assessment: What do teachers need to know and do? *Phi Delta Kappan, 89*(2), 140–145.

Herman, J. L., Osmundson, E., Ayala, C., Schneider, S., & Timms, M. (2006). *The nature and impact of teachers' formative assessment practices.* CSE Technical Report 703. Los Angeles: National Center for Research on Evaluation, Standards, and Student Testing. Available: http://www.cse.ucla.edu/products/reports/R703.pdf

Jacobs, H. H. (Ed.). (2004). *Getting results with curriculum mapping.* Alexandria, VA: ASCD.

Jensen, E. (2000). *Brain-based learning.* San Diego, CA: The Brain Store.

Joint Committee on Standards for Educational Evaluation. (2002). *Student evaluation standards.* Thousand Oaks, CA: Corwin Press.

King, J. R. (2003). *Teacher quality: Understanding the effectiveness of teacher attributes.* Washington, DC: Economic Policy Institute.

Margolis, H., & McCabe, P. P. (2006, March). Improving self-efficacy and motivation: What to do, what to say. *Intervention in School and Clinic, 41*(4), 218–227.

Marzano, R. J. (2003). *What works in schools: Translating research into action.* Alexandria, VA: ASCD.

Marzano, R. J. (2006). *Classroom assessment and grading that work.* Alexandria, VA: ASCD.

McMillan, J. H., & Schumacher, S. (1997). *Research in education: A conceptual introduction.* New York: Longman.

McMillan, J. H., & Workman, D. J. (1998). *Classroom assessment and grading practices: A review of the literature.* Richmond, VA: Metropolitan Educational Research Consortium. (ERIC Document Reproduction Service No., ED 453263)

Muir, M. (2001, November). What engages underachieving middle school students in learning? *Middle School Journal, 33*(2), 37–43.

National Center for Research on Evaluation, Standards, and Student Testing. (2001). *Glossary.* Available: http://www.cse.ucla.edu/resources/glossary.htm

National Council on Measurement in Education. (1995). *Code of professional responsibilities in educational measurement.* Madison, WI: Author. Available: http://www.ncme.org/about/documents.cfm

National Forum on Assessment. (1995). *Principles and indicators for student assessment systems.* Boston: FairTest Publications.

National Research Council. (2003). *Assessment in support of instruction and learning.* Washington, DC: National Academy Press.

New Commission on the Skills of the American Workforce. (2008). *Tough choices or tough times.* San Francisco: Jossey-Bass.

O'Connor, K. (2007). *A repair kit for grading: 15 fixes for broken grades.* Portland, OR: Educational Testing Service.

Partnership for 21st Century Skills. (2009). *Framework for 21st century learning.* Available: http://www.21stcenturyskills.org

Pellegrino, J. W., Chudowsky, N., & Glaser, R. (Eds.). (2001). *Knowing what students know: The science and design of educational assessment.* Washington, DC: National Academy Press.

PlasmaLink Web Services. (2007). *Glossary of instructional strategies.* Available: http://glossary.plasmalink.com/glossary.html

Popham, W. J. (2008). *Transformative assessment.* Alexandria, VA: ASCD.

Rice, J. K. (2003). *Teacher quality: Understanding the effectiveness of teacher attributes.* Washington, DC: Economic Policy Institute.

Rubenstein, G. (2008). *Brain imagery supports the idea of diverse intelligences.* George Lucas Educational Foundation, Edutopia. Available: http://www.edutopia.org/multiple-intelligences-brain-research

Rudner, L. M., & Schafer, W. D. (Eds.). (2002). *What teachers need to know about assessment.* Washington, DC: National Education Association.

Ruiz-Primo, M. A., & Furtak, E. M. (2004). *Informal formative assessment of students' understanding of scientific inquiry.* Los Angeles: National Center for Research on Evaluation, Standards, and Student Testing.

Sadler, D. R. (1989, June). Formative assessment and the design of instructional systems. *Instructional Science, 18*(2), 119–144.

Scriven, M. (1967). The methodology of evaluation. In R. W. Tyler, R. M. Gagné, & M. Scriven (Eds.), *Perspectives of curriculum evaluation* (pp. 39–83). Chicago: Rand McNally.

Sebba, J., Crick, R. D., Yu, G., Lawson, H., Harlen, W., & Durant, K. (2008). *Systematic review of research evidence of the impact on students in secondary schools of self and peer assessment.* I Research Evidence in Education Library series. London: EPPI-Centre, Social Science Research Unit, Institute of Education, University of London. Available: http://eppi.ioe.ac.uk/cms/Default.aspx?tabid=2415

Senge, P. (2000). *Schools that learn: A fifth discipline fieldbook for educators, parents, and everyone who cares about education.* New York: Doubleday.

Shepard, L. A. (2000). The role of assessment in a learning culture. *Educational Researcher, 29*(7), 4–14.

Stiggins, R. J. (2001). *The unfulfilled promise of classroom assessment.* Portland, OR: Assessment Training Institute.

Stiggins, R. J. (2002, June). Assessment crisis: The absence of assessment for learning. *Phi Delta Kappan, 83*(10), 758–765.

Stiggins, R. J., Arter, J., Chappuis, S., & Chappuis, J. (2004). *Classroom assessment for student learning: Doing it right—using it well.* Portland, OR: Assessment Training Institute.

Stiggins, R. J., & Popham, W. J. (2008). *Assessing student affect related to assessment for learning.* Washington, DC: Council of Chief State School Officers.

Tomlinson, C. A. (2007). *Differentiated instruction: Separating the wheat from chaff.* Paper presented at the 67th Annual Conference of ASCD, Anaheim, CA.

University of Pennsylvania (2009, March 28). Visual learners convert words to pictures in the brain and vice versa, says psychology study. *Science Daily.* Available: http://www.sciencedaily.com/releases/2009/03/090325091834.htm

Vygotsky, L. S. (1978). *Mind and society: The development of higher psychological processes.* Cambridge, MA: Harvard University Press.

Wiggins, G., & McTighe, J. (1998). *Understanding by design.* Alexandria, VA: ASCD.

Wiliam, D., Lee, C., Harrison, C., & Black, P. (2004) Teachers developing assessment for learning: Impact on student achievement. *Assessment in Education: Principles, Policy & Practice, 11*(1), 49–65.

Wormeli, R. (2006a). Differentiated assessment and grading. Web seminar presented October 19, 2006, at http://www.winsc.org/diff_assessment.htm

Wormeli, R. (2006b). *Fair isn't always equal: Assessing and grading in the differentiated classroom.* Portland, ME: Stenhouse.

Acknowledgments

This book was possible only through the efforts, support, and feedback of many people.

I give deepest thanks to my family, who keep the wind in my sails. My son, Andrew, has become my compass, and my daughter, Casey, continually reminds me that with time, anything is possible.

My thanks also go to the teachers and staff at Montville High School and Tyl Middle School, who provided many ideas for the book, particularly Laureen Anthony, who made preliminary edits. The Montville Public Schools administration gave valuable support and encouragement. I am indebted to all the teachers who provided formative assessment data on my formative assessment workshops and generously shared their thoughts and experiences with me. My doctoral cohort showed unlimited patience with my fervor for assessment. They have become friends and supporters on whom I depend for insight.

I thank Genny Ostertag and Katie Martin at ASCD for the tireless efforts that helped me navigate the way to the completion of this book.

And I thank my husband, Eric, for his infinite determination and lessons in *sisu*.

Index

The letter *f* following a page number denotes a figure, and the letter *d* indicates a definition.

About the Author

Laura Greenstein has been an educator for 35 years. She has experience as a classroom teacher (pre-K to 12th grade), department chairperson, board of education member, and professional development specialist. She is also an adjunct professor at the University of Connecticut and the University of New Haven. Her years spent outside of public education in state, federal, and nonprofit organizations have expanded her outlook on education. She has also served on local, state, and university leadership committees.

Dr. Greenstein has a B.S. from the University of Connecticut, an M.S. from the State University of New York at Oneonta, her 6th year in Educational Administration from Sacred Heart University, and her Ed.D. from Johnson and Wales University.

She and her husband live in East Lyme, Connecticut, and spend as much time as feasible with their adult children, who live in San Francisco. You can reach Laura Greenstein by e-mail at lauragteacher@hotmail.com or by visiting assessmentnetwork.net.

Related ASCD Resources: Formative Assessment

At the time of publication, the following ASCD resources were available (ASCD stock numbers appear in parentheses). For up-to-date information about ASCD resources, go to www.ascd.org. You can search the complete archives of *Educational Leadership* at http://www.ascd.org/el.

Multimedia
Formative Assessment Strategies for Every Classroom (2nd Ed.): An ASCD Action Tool by Susan M. Brookhart (#111005)

Online Professional Development
Formative Assessment: The Basics (#PD09OC69). Visit the ASCD website (www.ascd.org).

Print Products
Advancing Formative Assessment in Every Classroom: A Guide for Instructional Leaders by Connie M. Moss and Susan M. Brookhart (#109031)
Checking for Understanding: Formative Assessment Techniques for Your Classroom by Douglas Fisher and Nancy Frey (#107023)
Exploring Formative Assessment (The Professional Learning Community Series) by Susan M. Brookhart (#109038)
Transformative Assessment by W. James Popham (#108018)

Video
Formative Assessment in Content Areas (series of three 25-minute DVDs, each with a professional development program) (#609034)
Formative Assessment in Content Areas – Elementary School (one 25-minute DVD with a professional development program) (#609098)
Formative Assessment in Content Areas – Middle School (one 25-minute DVD with a professional development program) (#609099)
Formative Assessment in Content Areas – High School (one 25-minute DVD with a professional development program) (#609100)
The Power of Formative Assessment to Advance Learning (series of three 25- to 30-minute DVDs, with a comprehensive user guide) (#608066)

![THE WHOLE CHILD] The Whole Child Initiative helps schools and communities create learning environments that allow students to be healthy, safe, engaged, supported, and challenged. To learn more about other books and resources that relate to the whole child, visit www.wholechildeducation.org.

For more information: send e-mail to member@ascd.org; call 1-800-933-2723 or 703-578-9600, press 2; send a fax to 703-575-5400; or write to Information Services, ASCD, 1703 N. Beauregard St., Alexandria, VA 22311-1714 USA.